PREFACE

1. Scope

This publication provides joint doctrine for planning, executing, and assessing joint forcible entry operations.

2. Purpose

This publication has been prepared under the direction of the Chairman of the Joint Chiefs of Staff. It sets forth joint doctrine to govern the activities and performance of the Armed Forces of the US in joint operations and provides the doctrinal basis for US military coordination with other US Government departments and agencies during operations, and for US military involvement in multinational operations. It provides military guidance for the exercise of authority by combatant commanders and other joint force commanders (JFCs) and prescribes joint doctrine for operations, education, and training. It provides military guidance for use by the Armed Forces in preparing their appropriate plans. It is not the intent of this publication to restrict the authority of the JFC from organizing the force and executing the mission in a manner the JFC deems most appropriate to ensure unity of effort in the accomplishment of the overall objective.

3. Application

a. Joint doctrine established in this publication applies to the Joint Staff, commanders of combatant commands, subunified commands, joint task forces, subordinate components of these commands, and the Services.

b. The guidance in this publication is authoritative; as such, this doctrine will be followed except when, in the judgment of the commander, exceptional circumstances dictate otherwise. If conflicts arise between the contents of this publication and the contents of Service publications, this publication will take precedence unless the Chairman of the Joint Chiefs of Staff, normally in coordination with the other members of the Joint Chiefs of Staff, has provided more current and specific guidance. Commanders of forces operating as part of a multinational (alliance or coalition) military command should follow multinational doctrine and procedures ratified by the US. For doctrine and procedures not ratified by the US, commanders should evaluate and follow the multinational command's doctrine and procedures, where applicable and consistent with US law, regulations, and doctrine.

For the Chairman of the Joint Chiefs of Staff:

CURTIS M. SCAPARROTTI
Lieutenant General, U.S. Army
Director, Joint Staff

Intentionally Blank

- **Updated the discussion of information environment, information-related capabilities, cyberspace operations, and information superiority in accordance with changes to joint doctrine.**

- **Revised the definition of air assault, airborne assault, airhead, assault phase, lodgment, and vertical envelopment.**

- **Added discussion of operational access.**

- **Expanded the discussion of forcible entry to include amphibious raids.**

- **Added discussion on employment of special operations forces throughout the joint publication (JP).**

- **Modified or added several illustrations to conform to changes in the text, illustrate current capabilities, or clarify information in the body of the JP.**

- **Revised the discussion on command and control of the different types of forcible entry operations (airborne, air, and amphibious assault).**

- **Deleted paragraphs that cover material now found in JP 3-02, *Amphibious Operations*.**

- **Updated discussion of intelligence, surveillance, and reconnaissance, and joint intelligence preparation of the operational environment.**

- **Clarified the nomenclature and roles of specific types of units (example – the US Air Force combat communications groups).**

Intentionally Blank

TABLE OF CONTENTS

- **Presents the Principles of Joint Forcible Entry Operations and Forcible Entry Capabilities**

- **Explains the Command and Control of Joint Forcible Entry Operations**

- **Covers Planning**

- **Describes Forcible Entry Operations Are Conducted and the Phasing of Forcible Entry Operations**

- **Provides Logistical Planning Considerations for Joint Forcible Entry Operations**

Introduction

Joint Forcible Entry Operations

Joint forcible entry operations seize and hold lodgments against armed opposition. A lodgment is a designated area in a hostile or potentially hostile operational area that, when seized and held, makes the continuous landing of troops and materiel possible and provides maneuver space for subsequent operations (a lodgment may be an airhead, a beachhead, or a combination thereof). Forcible entry demands careful planning and thorough preparation; synchronized, violent, and rapid execution; and leader initiative at every level to deal with friction, chance, and opportunity.

United States National Military Strategy and Joint Forcible Entry Operations

To be credible both as a deterrent and as a viable military option for policy enforcement, the Armed Forces of the US must be capable of deploying and fighting to gain access to geographical areas controlled by forces hostile to US interests. Swift and decisive victory in these cases requires forcible entry and the ability to surge follow-on forces.

Principles for Forcible Entry Operational Success

The principles of forcible entry are: achieve surprise, control of the air, control of space, electromagnetic spectrum management, operations in the information environment, sea control, isolate the lodgment, gain and maintain access, neutralize enemy forces within the lodgment, expand the lodgment, manage the impact of environmental factors, and integrate supporting operations.

Operational Applications of
Forcible Entry Operations

A forcible entry operation may be the joint force commander's (JFC's) opening move to seize the initiative. For example, a JFC might direct **friendly forces to seize and hold an airhead or a beachhead** to facilitate the continuous landing of troops and materiel and expand the maneuver space needed to conduct follow-on operations. Forcible entry operations during the dominate phase of an operation or campaign may be used for the following purposes: a coup de main, conducting operational movement and maneuver to attain positional advantage, or as a military deception.

Forcible Entry Capabilities

The Armed Forces of the US conduct forcible entry operations using various capabilities including: **amphibious assault, amphibious raid, airborne assault, air assault, and any combination thereof.** Based upon mission analysis, joint intelligence preparation of the environment (JIPOE), and the joint operation planning process; these operations may be used singularly or in combination. Forcible entry operations may employ single or multiple entry points.

Multinational Considerations

Forcible entry operations with multinational partners are planned and conducted much the same as a US joint force operation. Multinational forces may bring additional capabilities and capacity to forcible entry operations but normally require careful attention to integration.

Command and Control

Force Employment

The JFC should determine the forcible entry capability or combination of capabilities needed to accomplish the mission. Unity of command is vital when amphibious, airborne, air assault, and special operations are combined. All elements of the joint force and supporting commands should understand the commander's intent, concept of operations (CONOPS), scheme of maneuver, and coordination requirements.

Organization of the Forcible Entry Operational Area

JFCs establish and maintain access to provide a forward presence, establish and maintain forward (intermediate) basing (to include availability of airfields), demonstrate freedom of navigation, and conduct military engagement, security cooperation, and deterrence operations and activities. The amphibious objective area is an area of land, sea, and airspace, assigned by a JFC to the amphibious force to conduct amphibious operations. The joint special operations area is an area of land, sea, and airspace, assigned by a JFC to the commander of a joint special operations (SO) force to conduct SO activities. The airspace control area for the forcible entry operation is that airspace laterally defined by **the boundaries that delineate the operational area.**

Command Relationships for Forcible Entry Operations

When conducting forcible entry operations into an area where special operations forces are already employed, it is imperative that both conventional and special operations synchronize and coordinate their respective operations/missions.

The combatant commander may organize the forcible entry force as a subordinate joint task force, or the forcible entry force may be organized from an existing component. Designating a joint force functional component commander for a particular functional area allows resolution of joint issues at the functional component level and enhances component interaction at that level. Based on the JFC's guidance, the forcible entry operation may be conducted by functional component commanders. If the forcible entry operation is an amphibious assault, it will include air and land assaults that originate from the sea. Normally, a support relationship is established between the commander, amphibious task force and commander, landing force by the JFC or establishing authority. If the forcible entry operation is an airborne assault, it will be delivered by airlift forces from either the continental United States, an intermediate staging base, or a theater airbase. The airborne task force commander will normally exercise responsibility for the airlift plan, to include priority of airdrop and airland sorties, the preparatory fires plan, and the ground tactical plan in the airhead. Forcible entry operations employing a combination of airborne, air assault, special operations forces (SOF), and amphibious forces (to include multinational forces with these capabilities), **may be under the command of the JFC or a Service or functional component commander** and must be closely coordinated.

Air Defense Command and Control

The joint force is particularly vulnerable to attacks by enemy aircraft or surface-to-surface missiles during the early stages of a forcible entry. The primary objectives for air and missile defense operations are to assist in gaining air superiority and protecting the assault force. The area air defense commander is responsible for integrating the joint force air defense effort.

Communications

Communications systems supporting forcible entry operations must be interoperable, agile, trusted, and shared. Interoperability can be achieved through commonality, compatibility, standardization, and liaison.

Rules of Engagement

Rules of engagement (ROE) ensure actions, especially force employment, are consistent with military objectives, domestic and international law, and national policy. The challenge for a JFC is to ensure that the ROE for a forcible entry operation provides the commander with the flexibility to accomplish the mission, while assuring adherence to political, legal, operational, and diplomatic factors the force may encounter.

Planning

Forcible Entry and the Joint Planning Process

During deliberate planning, the operation plan or concept plan, and supporting annexes, for an operation or campaign are prepared. This includes forcible entry operation requirements. Forcible entry operations require extensive JIPOE. Forcible entry will require well-trained and well-prepared joint forces capable of executing operations on short-notice. It is essential that all key elements associated with the operation are included in the planning forum from the onset.

Forcible Entry Planning Considerations	In analyzing a forcible entry operation, the JFC and staff consider lodgment terrain and infrastructure, with a critical eye on the ability to support follow-on operations, and forces available including multinational and indigenous. In the development of a forcible entry course of action, five phases are addressed: preparation and deployment, assault, stabilization of the lodgment, introduction of follow-on forces, and termination or transition.

Operations

Integration and Synchronization	In order to integrate, synchronize, and confirm the timing of an operation, the JFC may choose to conduct a rehearsal. The decision to conduct rehearsals will be influenced by the time available and by operations security (OPSEC) considerations.
Forcible Entry Operations Phases	Forcible entry operations are normally conducted during the "seize the initiative" or "dominate" phase of a joint operation. Within the context of these phases established by a higher-level JFC, the forcible entry operation commander may establish additional phases that fit the forcible entry CONOPS.
Preparation and Deployment (Phase I)	Forcible entry operations are conducted by organizations whose force structures permit rapid deployment into the objective area.
Assault (Phase II)	Phase II begins with **joint force assaults** to seize initial objectives in the lodgment and concludes with the **consolidation of those objectives.**
Stabilization of the Lodgment (Phase III)	Stabilization involves **securing the lodgment** to protect the force and ensure the continuous landing of personnel and materiel, **organizing the lodgment** to support the increasing flow of forces and logistic resource requirements, and **expanding the lodgment** as required to support the joint force in preparing for and executing follow-on operations.

Introduction of Follow-on Forces (Phase IV)

Follow-on forces provide the JFC with **increased flexibility to conduct operations as required by operational conditions.** In some operations and campaigns, the follow-on forces will conduct ground offensive operations to link up with forces in the lodgment.

Termination or Transition Operations (Phase V)

The transition from a forcible entry operation to subsequent operations or termination must be an integral part of the planning phase of the joint deployment process. **A successful forcible entry operation is completed in one of two ways:** attainment of the campaign objectives (termination); or completion of the operational objectives wherein a lodgment is established for follow-on combat operations (transition).

Special Operations Forces

SOF may be employed prior to forcible entry operations to collect intelligence, seize key terrain, organize and train guerrilla forces, and conduct other activities that facilitate the introduction of conventional forces. In the execution stages of a forcible entry operation, SOF can seize objectives, interdict targets (especially those that can severely disrupt the assault to open entry points), and conduct other operations to support the main force.

Fires

In forcible entry operations, the initial assault forces are building combat power in the operational area from nothing as quickly as possible. They will normally have very minimal or no artillery support available for fire support in the early stages of the operation. Fires from aircraft (manned and unmanned) and/or naval platforms (surface/subsurface) take on added importance to compensate for the lack of artillery.

Intelligence Support and Considerations

The JFC uses intelligence to decide what, why, when, where, and how to attack; determine forcible entry capabilities needed and task organization required to seize initial objective(s); support targeting and combat assessment; and anticipate future operations.

Information Operations

Information operations (IO) is a key part of setting the conditions for forcible entry operational success; IO efforts will be central to achieving surprise and isolating the lodgment and will also be an important enabler for gaining control of the operational environment and neutralizing enemy forces. OPSEC and military deception, combined with the other information-related capabilities will be the heart of achieving operational and tactical surprise during the forcible entry operation.

Logistics

Specific Logistic Considerations for Supporting Forcible Entry Operations

Logistic planning must account for early resupply of initial assault forces as these forces will generally be employed with limited on-hand capacities. As applied to military operations and forcible entry operations specifically, logistic services comprise the support capabilities that collectively enable the US to rapidly provide sustainment for military forces in order to achieve the envisioned end state of the operation or larger campaign

Phase I (Preparation and Deployment) Logistic Planning Considerations

Phase I logistic planning considerations include:

• Determine air, land, and sea line of communications requirements to support forcible entry and subsequent operations.

• Determine logistic factors and establish airhead and beachhead resupply responsibility.

Phase II (Assault) Logistic Planning Considerations

Phase II logistic planning considerations include:

• Analyze potential lodgment area to ensure continuous air and sea landing of personnel, equipment, and logistic resources, as well as availability of facilities.

• Provide adequate medical support and evacuation to support concurrent or integrated assaults by amphibious, airborne, air assault, and SOF.

Phase III (Stabilization of the Lodgment) Logistic Planning Considerations

Phase III logistic planning considerations include:

- Project and/or resolve restrictions and/or limitations in the capability to support force flow.

- Develop provisions to clear reinforcing supplies and equipment from off-load points.

- Analyze requirements to expand the lodgment with regard to maximum on ground capabilities, throughput, and infrastructure.

Phase IV (Introduction of Follow-on Forces) Logistic Planning Considerations

Phase IV logistic planning considerations include:

- Identify mission support requirements for follow-on operations.

- Begin maritime pre-positioning force and Army pre-positioned stocks afloat operations.

- Plan for reconstitution and redeployment of the assault force for follow-on operations.

Phase V (Termination or Transition Operations) Logistic Planning Considerations

Phase V logistic planning considerations include:

- Redeploy and/or reconstitute assault forces as appropriate.

- Plan for preparing the force for follow-on, out-of-area operations, such as redeployment to another geographical area.

CONCLUSION

This publication provides joint doctrine for planning, executing, and assessing joint forcible entry operations.

CHAPTER I
INTRODUCTION

"As a global power with global interests, the United States must maintain the credible capability to project military force into any region of the world in support of those interests. This includes the ability to project force both into the global commons to ensure their use and into foreign territory as required."

Joint Operational Access Concept (JOAC), 17 January 2012

1. Forcible Entry

a. Joint forcible entry operations seize and hold lodgments against armed opposition. A lodgment is a designated area in a hostile or potentially hostile operational area that, when seized and held, makes the continuous landing of troops and materiel possible and provides maneuver space for subsequent operations (a lodgment may be an airhead, a beachhead, or a combination thereof). The lodgment and the means of seizing will depend upon the objectives of the operation or campaign. In most operations, forcible entry secures the lodgment as a base for subsequent operations. It often has facilities and infrastructure if the joint commander plans to use the lodgment to receive large follow-on forces and logistics. In some operations, seizure of the lodgment may be the primary objective, and its retention lasts only until the mission is complete, at which time the assaulting forces withdraw. Forcible entry operations are inherently risky and always joint. Forcible entry demands careful planning and thorough preparation; synchronized, violent, and rapid execution; and leader initiative at every level to deal with friction, chance, and opportunity. See Figure I-1.

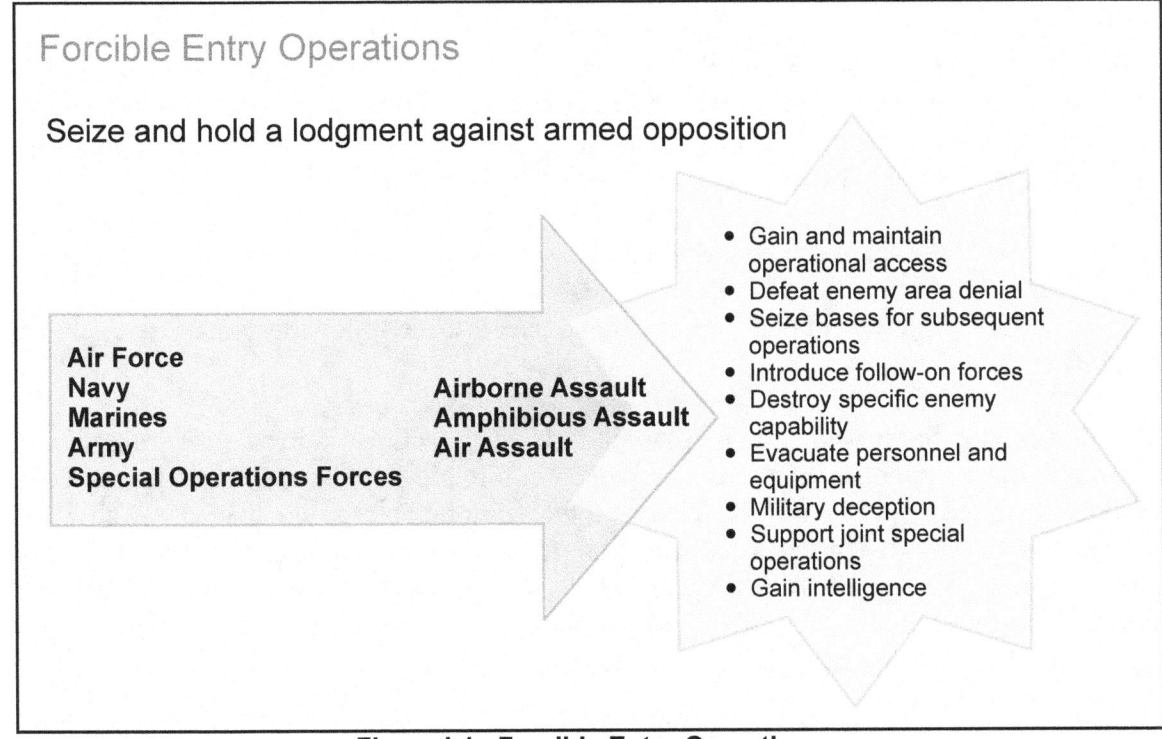

Figure I-1. Forcible Entry Operations

b. The US seeks to gain and maintain operational access in areas of strategic importance throughout the world. Operational access is the ability to project military force into an operational area with sufficient freedom of action to accomplish the mission. Operational access is the joint force contribution to a whole of government approach to assured access that includes, for example, the diplomatic and economic instruments of national power. Access also includes the unhindered use of the global commons, in turn, are: areas of air, sea, space, and cyberspace that belong to no one state, and select sovereign territory. Forcible entry is a military aspect of operational access that may be applied when diplomatic and other means have failed.

c. **Forcible entry operations are joint in nature.** There are many Service and functional component-unique forcible entry capabilities, techniques, and procedures the Nation has developed since World War II, primarily consisting of amphibious assault, amphibious raid, airborne assault, air assault, and special operations (SO). Despite these Service-oriented capabilities, techniques, and procedures, forcible entry operations are inherently joint as evidenced by the need for using resources (e.g., command and control [C2], transportation, sustainment) from all elements of the Department of Defense (DOD) and often other resources (e.g., multinational and other government departments and agencies.)

2. United States National Military Strategy and Joint Forcible Entry Operations

a. The National Military Strategy establishes four supporting military objectives: counter violent extremism, deter and defeat aggression, strengthen international and regional security, and shape the future force.

b. To be credible both as a deterrent and as a viable military option for policy enforcement, the Armed Forces of the US must be capable of deploying and fighting to gain access to geographical areas controlled by forces hostile to US interests. Swift and decisive victory in these cases requires forcible entry and the ability to surge follow-on forces. Alerting rapid deployment forces for employment or moving forces toward the area of the crisis is a show of force that is diplomatically significant in a strategic context.

3. Principles for Forcible Entry Operational Success

To set favorable conditions for operational success, the following principles apply for forcible entry operations:

a. **Achieve Surprise.** Planners should strive to achieve surprise regarding exact objectives, times, methods, and forces employed in forcible entry operations. The degree of surprise required depends on the nature of the operation to be conducted. **Achieving surprise is usually dependent upon multiple factors to include information operations (IO), operations security (OPSEC), military deception (MILDEC), and operational tempo.** Surprise is not a necessary condition for operational success (particularly when the force has overwhelming superiority), but it can significantly reduce operational risk.

OPERATION OVERLORD—France, 1944

The D-DAY invasion on 6 June 1944 was preceded by counterintelligence, military deception, and operations security efforts unprecedented in scope. As early as 1940, the British initiated actions to sink or capture the German weather ships and submarines stationed in the North Atlantic. This continued throughout the war. German agents operating in Great Britain were eliminated or "turned," and almost all of the intelligence they sent to Germany was compromised. Prior to the invasion, Allied bombers struck targets throughout the possible invasion areas, while avoiding undue concentration on the Normandy Peninsula. Allied air forces denied the German air force any aerial reconnaissance over the assembly areas and ports used for the invasion. Entire English civilian communities were removed from staging and embarkation areas and the invasion troops themselves kept in isolation. An elaborate military deception operation maintained the ruse that the main invasion would strike the Pas de Calais area instead of Normandy. On the night of the invasion, false parachute drops were staged in areas outside of the invasion area.

The effect on German defensive operations was critical. At the strategic level, the Germans expected the invasion in the spring of 1944. Lack of operational intelligence forced the Germans to defend all the possible invasion areas in western France, and kept most mobile reserves away from the invasion beaches in a central location. Allied air and French partisans delayed them from striking the lodgment until too late. The lack of accurate weather data led to erroneous weather forecasts for early June. Lacking air reconnaissance, the Germans kept powerful forces to defend the Pas de Calais, which the German Army assessed as most likely and most dangerous area.

Various Sources

b. **Control of the Air.** Counterair integrates offensive and defensive operations to attain and maintain a desired degree of air superiority and protection in the operational area. During forcible entry operations this is essential to **protect the force during periods of critical vulnerability,** and to **preserve lines of communications (LOCs).** At a minimum, the joint force must neutralize the enemy's offensive air and missile capability and air defenses to achieve local air superiority and protection over the planned lodgment. **The joint force controls the air through integrated and synchronized air and missile defense operations.** Air interdiction of enemy forces throughout the operational area enhances the simultaneity and depth of the forcible entry operation.

c. **Control of Space.** Space superiority allows the joint force commander (JFC) access to communications, weather, navigation, timing, remote sensing, and intelligence assets without prohibitive interference by the opposing force.

d. **Electromagnetic Spectrum Management.** Electromagnetic spectrum management operations are those interrelated functions of frequency management, host nation coordination, and joint spectrum interference resolution that together enable the planning, management, and execution of operations within the electromagnetic operational environment during all phases of military operations.

e. **Operations in the Information Environment.** Information superiority enables the primary mission objective and information-related activities within IO. Information-related capabilities include MILDEC, OPSEC, military information support operations, electronic warfare (EW), combat camera, public affairs (PA), key leader engagement, cyberspace operations (CO), and numerous additional tools and techniques. As our adversaries increase the sophistication of their operations, the criticality of gaining superiority in the information environment also increases.

For more information on information-related capabilities, see Joint Publication (JP) 3-0, Joint Operations, *and JP 3-13,* Information Operations.

f. **Sea Control.** Local maritime superiority is required to **project power ashore in support of the joint forcible entry operation and to protect sea lines of communications (SLOCs).** Protection of SLOCs enables the availability of logistic support required to sustain operations and support the transition to continuing operations by follow-on forces.

g. **Isolate the Lodgment.** The joint force **attacks or neutralizes any enemy capabilities with the potential to affect the establishment of the lodgment.** These capabilities include enemy ground, sea, and air forces that can be committed to react to joint force assaults, indirect fire systems, and theater missile systems that can range the lodgment, and related sensors, C2 systems, and digital networks.

h. **Gain and Maintain Access.** In any given operational area, numerous and diverse limitations to access will present themselves. Access may be restricted due to diplomatic, economic, military, or cultural factors. Ports, airfields, and infrastructures may also be physically limited.

(1) **Commander Considerations.** Commanders conducting forcible entry operations should leverage established basing, access, and security cooperation agreements as well as the regional expertise developed through pre-crisis engagement activities at the national, regional, and local levels.

(2) **Shaping Efforts.** When planning indicates a requirement for forcible entry, shaping efforts or activities focus on identifying and neutralizing an adversary's anti-access capabilities. This may require a change in intelligence, surveillance, and reconnaissance (ISR) priorities: for example, increasing surveillance and reconnaissance to locate natural and man-made impediments to entry operations. Shaping activities may involve MILDEC, OPSEC, and IO. However, all shaping should be balanced against the need for surprise. Other government departments and agencies and multinational partners may be vital to developing intelligence and gaining sufficient access to permit forcible entry.

(3) **Operational Access.** Operational access expands the degree to which the JFC may employ the range of joint capabilities within the operational area. Gaining and maintaining operational access depends upon numerous factors such as the nature of the operation or campaign, geography, the enemy's capability to deny access, proximity of friendly bases, and the joint capabilities available. Forcible entry operations are often the precursor to follow-on major operations. Land forces projected into the lodgment seize key terrain, and eliminate enemy anti-access capabilities. Air Force, Navy, and joint special operations forces (SOF) extend their reach and ability to neutralize the enemy's anti-access measures. Ultimately, the forcible entry may completely dislocate enemy defenses and allow the joint force to retain the initiative throughout the dominate phase. In some instances, forcible entry operations preclude enemy anti-access measures and seize the initiative. For example, Operation WATCHTOWER in August of 1942 seized the Japanese airfield on Guadalcanal and nearby seaplane base. This operation surprised the Japanese and completely disrupted Japanese plans to extend their strategic defensive perimeter and interdict SLOCs between the US and Australia.

i. **Neutralize Enemy Forces Within the Lodgment.** The joint force must neutralize enemy forces within the lodgment to **facilitate the establishment of airheads and beachheads** and to **provide for the immediate protection of the force.**

j. Planning considerations should include identification of enemy infrastructure which may be of value for future use by friendly forces. Limiting physical damage will lessen the time needed to rebuild.

k. **Expand the Lodgment.** The joint force quickly builds combat power in order to enhance security and the ability to respond to enemy counter attacks; enable continuous landing of troops and materiel; and facilitate transition to subsequent operations.

l. **Manage the Impact of Environmental Factors.** Managing the impact of environmental factors refers to overcoming the effect of land and sea obstacles; **anticipating, preventing, detecting, and mitigating adversary** use of chemical, biological, radiological, or nuclear (CBRN) weapons; and, determining **the impact of climate, weather, and other naturally occurring hazards.**

m. **Integrate Supporting Operations.** Surveillance operations, reconnaissance operations, IO, civil-military operations (CMO), SO are key to setting the conditions for forcible entry operational success. These enablers should be integrated into the operation at every stage from initial planning to transition.

4. Operational Applications of Forcible Entry Operations

Generally, joint operations and campaigns involve six phases, as illustrated in Figure I-2. The geographic combatant commander's (GCC's) vision of how a joint operation should unfold will drive decisions regarding the phasing of an operation. Within the context of the phases established by a GCC, subordinate JFCs and component commanders may establish additional phases that fit their concept of operations (CONOPS). A creditable threat of

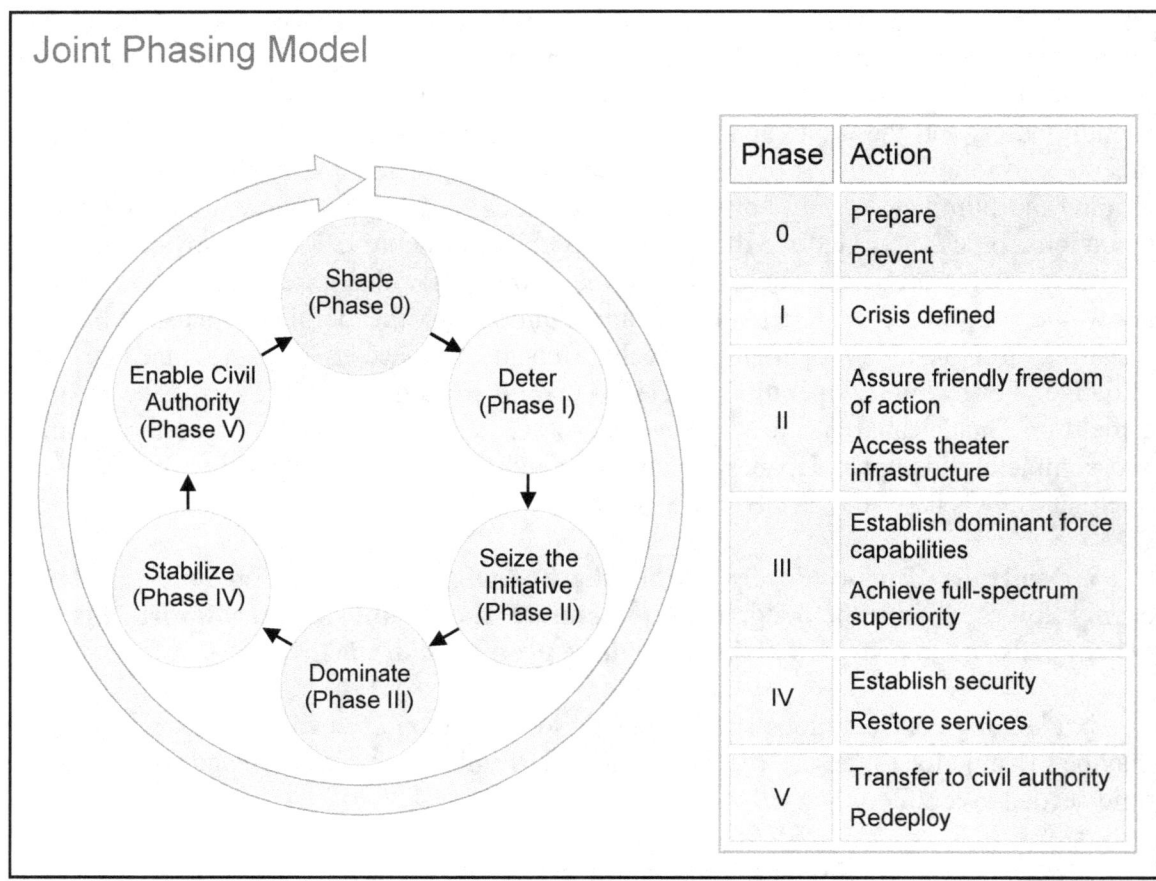

Figure I-2. Joint Phasing Model

forcible entry operations can be an effective deterrence and may be applicable in both phase 0 (Shape) and phase 1 (Deter). A forcible entry operation will normally be conducted during phases II (Seize the Initiative) or III (Dominate) of a joint operation.

a. **Seize the Initiative.** A forcible entry operation may be the JFC's opening move to seize the initiative. For example, a JFC might direct **friendly forces to seize and hold an airhead or a beachhead** to facilitate the continuous landing of troops and materiel and expand the maneuver space needed to conduct follow-on operations. The establishment of the lodgment, followed by the arrival and preparation of follow-on forces, usually marks the end of the forcible entry operations and a transition to further offensive operations. Operation CHROMITE (1950) is an example of forcible entry as a major operation with a campaign.

b. **Dominate.** Forcible entry operations during the dominate phase of an operation or campaign may be used for the following purposes: a coup de main, conducting operational movement and maneuver to attain positional advantage (see Operation CHROMITE [1950] vignette), or as a MILDEC.

OPERATION CHROMITE—Korea, 1950

On September 15, 1950, eighty three days after North Korea invaded South Korea, a joint command of the United States, Joint Task Force 7, initiated Operation CHROMITE by conducting an amphibious assault on the port of Inchon on Korea's west coast.

Operation CHROMITE took place on the heels of the retreat of the United States and Republic of Korea forces down the Korean Peninsula in June and July to an enclave on the peninsula's southern tip. The primary objectives were to land a large force behind the bulk of the North Korean People's Army (NKPA), recapture South Korea's capital, Seoul, cut NKPA logistic lines, and provide an "anvil" against which the US Eighth Army, attacking from the south, would crush the NKPA.

Joint Task Force 7 commenced operations at 0630 on September 15th with an assault against the critical island of Wolmi-Do following massive bombardment. By 1800 on September 16th, main landings on Inchon had secured a beachhead.

Various Sources

(1) **Coup de Main.** A forcible entry may be designed as a coup de main that will achieve decisive results. Often conducted by small forces conducting short duration, limited objective attacks against opponents with modest but still lethal capabilities, these operations are seldom studied in detail but may be the most likely type of forcible entry in the near future. Operation URGENT FURY (1983) and Operation JUST CAUSE (1989-90) are specific examples of the use of simultaneous operations overwhelming an enemy's ability to respond. The capitulation of enemy forces usually marks the end of the dominate phase of the operation and a transition to further operations within the stabilize and enable civil authority phases.

(2) **Military Deception.** The mere existence of a forcible entry capability may be used by the JFC in any phase as a show of force or to force enemy movement even without mounting a forcible entry operation, as with the amphibious demonstration during Operation DESERT STORM (1991).

For further information on phasing, refer to JP 3-0, Joint Operations, *and JP 5-0,* Joint Operation Planning.

5. **Forcible Entry Capabilities**

The Armed Forces of the US conduct forcible entry operations using various capabilities including: **amphibious assault, amphibious raid, airborne assault, air assault, and any combination thereof.** Based upon mission analysis, joint intelligence preparation of the environment (JIPOE), and the joint operation planning process (JOPP); these operations may be used singularly or in combination. Forcible entry operations may employ single or multiple entry points. In some cases, SOF will support the entry of conventional forces, but conventional forces may be used to seize a lodgment for support of SO missions. The forcible entry operation may include linkup and exploitation by ground maneuver from a separate location. Sustainment considerations may drive the requirement for a combination of capabilities and linkup requirements.

> **The Inchon amphibious assault (see Operation CHROMITE) established a lodgment on the west coast of Korea, simultaneously with the counteroffensive to break out of the Pusan Perimeter. The Pusan offensive involved the majority of United Nations ground forces. The amphibious force and forces from the Pusan area linked up in the vicinity of Seoul to continue the offensive.**
>
> *South to the Naktong, North to the Yalu,* Roy E. Appleman

a. **Amphibious Assault Operations.** An amphibious force (AF), composed of an amphibious task force (ATF) and a landing force (LF), together with other forces that are trained, organized, and equipped for amphibious operations, conducts littoral maneuver by vertical and/or surface means. AFs seek to exploit gaps in the adversary's defenses to secure key objectives associated with establishing a lodgment. In addition to serving as a forcible entry assault force, such forces are **capable of conducting follow-on operations** from the lodgment. AFs may also be inserted as a follow-on force. An AF with a forcible entry capability may be forward-deployed to quickly initiate or join other forces in a forcible entry operation or as a show of force. Support from the sea and projected ashore facilitates the rapid build-up of combat power to include the introduction of follow-on forces.

A US Navy Wasp Class Amphibious Assault Ship underway in the Pacific Ocean.

Appendix A, "Amphibious Assault Operations," and JP 3-02, Amphibious Operations, *provide more specifics on amphibious operations.*

b. **Airborne Assault Operations.** Airborne forces may be used as the **assault force or used in combination with other capabilities for a forcible entry;** or they may **conduct follow-on operations from a lodgment.** As an assault force, airborne forces parachute into the objective area to attack and eliminate armed resistance and secure designated objectives. Airborne forces may also be employed from a lodgment in additional joint combat operations appropriate to their training and equipment. Airborne forces offer the JFC an immediate forcible entry option since they can be launched directly from the continental US (CONUS) without the delays associated with acquiring intermediate staging bases (ISBs) or re-positioning of sea-based forces.

c. **Air Assault Operations.** Air assault forces execute forcible entries using **fixed- and rotary-wing aircraft.** Air assault forces can deploy from **land-based facilities** and **ships.** Fires from land and sea-based aircraft (manned and unmanned) and/or ships (surface/subsurface) take on added importance to compensate for the lack of field artillery. An air assault force may require the establishment of an ISB. These forces can rapidly project combat power throughout the depth of an operational area.
Appendix B, "Airborne and Air Assault Operations," provides more specifics on airborne and air assault operations.

d. **Special Operations.** SOF can execute forcible entries using a combination of fixed- and rotary-wing aircraft employing air land or airdrop procedures. Depending on threat and other circumstances, SOF can use alternate forms of infiltration. Routinely, SOF may require conventional support such as air refueling, close air support (CAS), EW, IO, etc. Normally, SOF forcible entry operations are of short duration to meet specific JFC objectives. For more information on SOF missions and capabilities, refer to JP, 3-05, *Special Operations.*

OPERATION ENDURING FREEDOM I, AFGHANISTAN, 2001

Although forcible entry is conducted with the expectation and due preparation for armed opposition, prudent commanders have always sought to conduct such operations in a manner that avoids enemy defenses to the greatest extent possible. Major General Alexander A. Vandergrift, United States Marine Corps, clearly articulated that view in his 1943 assessment of operations in the Solomon Islands. He noted that a comparison of the several landings leads to the inescapable conclusion that landings should not be attempted in the face of organized resistance if, by any combination of march or maneuver, it is possible to land unopposed within striking distance of the objective.

The beginning of Operation ENDURING FREEDOM in 2001 provides perhaps the best illustration of this idea. Initial campaign actions involved special operations forces and US airpower teamed up with local militias to fight al-Qaeda and the Taliban in northern Afghanistan.

> **While these actions were underway, plans were taking shape to open a second front in southern Afghanistan. On 25 November 2001 the 15th Marine Expeditionary Unit, operating from the USS PELELIU Amphibious Ready Group in the North Arabian Sea, conducted the longest ship-to-objective maneuver in history, moving 400 miles inland to seize the desert airstrip south of Kandahar.**
>
> **Renamed Forward Operating Base Rhino, this lodgment supported the introduction of additional joint forces via inter-theater airlift. It enabled the isolation and seizure of Kandahar, the last political and military stronghold of the Taliban regime. Merging the complementary strengths of sea power and airpower to great advantage, this approach succeeding in projecting US maneuver forces deep into hostile territory in a manner that was fast and effective while allowing the joint force commander to retain the initiative regarding when and where to give battle.**
>
> **Various Sources**

6. Multinational Considerations

a. Forcible entry operations with multinational partners are planned and conducted much the same as a US joint force operation. However, there may be aspects of a multinational forces' organization, or procedures that the commander of a US joint force needs to consider. Attaining unity of effort through unity of command for a multinational operation may not be politically feasible, but it should be a goal. There must be a common understanding among all national forces of the overall aim of the multinational force and the plan to achieve that intent. Commanders and staffs at all levels should also account for differences in partner nations' laws, weapons, equipment, technology, culture, politics, and language.

b. Multinational forces may bring additional capabilities and capacity to forcible entry operations but normally require careful attention to integration. To optimize these multinational forces the JFC and component commanders may need to employ unplanned for liaison teams to multiple disperse locations. Additional training and rehearsal may also be required to fully integrate the multinational elements into the joint forces. Key to optimizing the participation of multinational forces is understanding their capabilities and coordinating and integrating them into planning and execution as quickly as possible. This may include understanding national limitations placed on contributing forces as well as the experience and morale of individual units. Both US and multinational forces may require training and education prior to employment as a joint force and the exchange of multiple liaison officers.

For additional information, see JP 3-16, Multinational Operations. *For information specific to US participation in North Atlantic Treaty Organization operations, see the appropriate Allied joint publications and Allied tactical publications.*

CHAPTER II
COMMAND AND CONTROL

> ". . . a superior command system may serve as a force multiplier and compensate for weaknesses . . . such as numerical inferiority or the politically induced need to leave the initiative to the enemy."
>
> **Martin van Creveld**
> ***Command in War*, 1985**

1. Purpose

This chapter provides guidance on the employment options, organization of the forcible entry operational area, command relationships, and major C2 functions that support the conduct of joint forcible entry operations.

2. Force Employment

The JFC should determine the forcible entry capability or combination of capabilities needed to accomplish the mission. Unity of command is vital when amphibious, airborne, air assault, and SO are combined. Forcible entry is a complex operation and should therefore be kept as simple as possible in concept. All elements of the joint force and supporting commands should understand the commander's intent, CONOPS, scheme of maneuver, and coordination requirements.

a. If the decision is made to use a combination of forcible entry capabilities to seize a lodgment, the JFC also decides whether to conduct the forcible entries as concurrent or integrated operations. **Concurrent operations** occur when a combination of amphibious raid or assault, airborne, and/or air assault forcible entry operations are conducted simultaneously, but as **distinct operations with separate operational areas and objectives** (e.g., the amphibious assault operation around Pearls Airport and the airborne operation at Point Salinas in Grenada during Operation URGENT FURY). **Integrated forcible entry operations** result when amphibious raid or assault, airborne, and/or air assault forcible entries are **conducted simultaneously within the same operational area and with objectives that are mutually supporting** (e.g., the airborne operation in support of the amphibious assault landings in Normandy during Operation OVERLORD).

b. **The distinction between concurrent and integrated operations** has implications for organizing forces, establishing command relationships, and applying force to accomplish the mission. Factors that may impact the establishing authority's decision include the following:

(1) The responsibility for the preponderance of the mission.

(2) Time, phase, and duration of the operation.

(3) Force capabilities.

(4) Threat.

(5) C2 capabilities.

(6) The operational environment.

(7) Recommendations from subordinate commanders.

(8) Follow-on missions, anticipated operations, or transition considerations based upon the objective(s) of the overall operation or larger campaign plan.

(9) The diplomatic and politico-military environment.

3. Organization of the Forcible Entry Operational Area

a. **Maintaining Operational Area Access.** JFCs establish and maintain access to provide a forward presence, establish and maintain forward (intermediate) basing (to include availability of airfields), demonstrate freedom of navigation, and conduct military engagement, security cooperation, and deterrence operations and activities. This effort may also involve maintenance of intertheater air and sea LOCs.

b. **Amphibious Objective Area.** The Amphibious Objective Area (AOA) is an area of land, sea, and airspace, assigned by a JFC to the AF to conduct amphibious operations. The AOA is normally specified in the initiating directive. This area must be of sufficient size to ensure accomplishment of the AF's mission and must provide sufficient area for conducting necessary sea, air, and land operations.

See JP 3-02, Amphibious Operations, *for more information on AOAs.*

c. **Joint Special Operations Area.** The Joint Special Operations Area (JSOA) is an area of land, sea, and airspace, assigned by a JFC to the commander of a joint SO force to conduct SO activities. The JFC may establish a JSOA when geographic boundaries between SOF and conventional forces are the most suitable control measures. Establishment of a JSOA for SOF to conduct operations provides a control measure and assists in the prevention of fratricide. The commander, joint special operations task force (CDRJSOTF) may also request the establishment of a JSOA. When a JSOA is designated, the CDRJSOTF is the supported commander within the designated JSOA. The CDRJSOTF may further assign a specific area or sector within the JSOA to a subordinate commander for mission execution. The scope and duration of the SOF mission, operational environment, and politico-military considerations all influence the number, composition, and sequencing of SOF deployed into a JSOA. It may be limited in size to accommodate a discrete direct action mission or may be extensive enough to allow a continuing broad range of unconventional warfare (UW) operations.

d. **Airspace Control Area.** The airspace control area for the forcible entry operation is that airspace laterally defined by **the boundaries that delineate the operational area.** This airspace may include sub-areas. This airspace may entail any operational area and is a means of planning and dividing responsibility. While an operational area is in existence, airspace control within the operational area is in accordance with JFC guidance, the airspace control plan, and airspace control order.

e. **Control and Coordination Measures.** Control and coordination of forcible entry operations pose a particularly difficult challenge to all elements of the joint force. In addressing this challenge, the JFCs and appropriate commanders may employ various control and coordination measures that will facilitate the execution of operations and, at the same time, protect the force to the greatest possible degree. These measures include, but are not limited to, boundaries that circumscribe operational areas; control measures to facilitate joint force maneuver; fire support coordination measures (FSCMs); and airspace coordinating measures.

See JP 3-0, Joint Operations, for guidance on organizing the operational area.

4. Command Relationships for Forcible Entry Operations

a. **Joint Force Commander Authority.** JFCs have full authority to assign missions, redirect efforts, and direct coordination among subordinate commanders. JFCs should allow Service tactical and operational groupings to function generally as they are organized and trained.

b. **Combatant Commanders.** The combatant commander (CCDR) may organize the forcible entry force as a subordinate joint task force (JTF), or the forcible entry force may be organized from an existing component. An initiating directive will provide guidance on command relationships and other pertinent instructions for the duration of the forcible entry operation.

See JP 3-33, Joint Task Force Headquarters, for guidance.

c. **Functional Component Commanders.** The multiple complex tasks confronting the JFC may challenge the JFC's span of control and ability to oversee and influence each task. Designating a joint force functional component commander for a particular functional area allows resolution of joint issues at the functional component level and enhances component interaction at that level. In a large operation, delegating control of the forcible entry operation to a functional component commander will permit the JFC to focus on other responsibilities in the operational area. Based on the JFC's guidance, the forcible entry operation may be conducted by functional component commanders. If organized under functional lines, the following information is relevant:

(1) **Joint Force Land Component Commander.** The joint force land component commander (JFLCC's) overall responsibilities and roles are to plan, coordinate, and employ designated forces/capabilities for joint land operations in support of the JFC's CONOPS. The JFLCC will normally command forcible entry operations that involve airborne assaults

or air assaults that originate from land bases, and will typically designate the commander, airborne/air assault force (CAF).

(2) **Joint Force Maritime Component Commander.** The joint force maritime component commander (JFMCC's) overall responsibilities and roles are to plan, coordinate, and employ designated forces/capabilities for joint maritime operations in support of the JFC's CONOPS.

(3) **Joint Force Air Component Commander.** The joint force air component commander (JFACC) synchronizes and integrates the actions of assigned, attached, and supporting air capabilities/forces in time, space, and purpose in support of the JFC's CONOPS. The JFACC must closely coordinate with the supported functional component commander or JTF commander to establish airspace control and air defense plans in support of the forcible entry operation as discussed below.

d. **Amphibious Task Force and Landing Force Commanders.** If the forcible entry operation is an amphibious assault, it will include air and land assaults that originate from the sea. The JFC will organize the AF in such a way as to best accomplish the mission based on the CONOPS. The command relationships established among the commander, amphibious task force (CATF), commander, landing force (CLF), and other designated commanders of the AF is an important decision. An establishing directive is essential to ensure unity of effort within the AF. Normally, a support relationship is established between the CATF and CLF by the JFC or establishing authority.

For additional information on C2 by functional component commanders, see JP 3-30, Command and Control for Joint Air Operations, *JP 3-31,* Command and Control for Joint Land Operations, *and JP 3-32,* Command and Control for Joint Maritime Operations. *For further details on amphibious command relationships, see JP 3-02,* Amphibious Operations.

e. **Airborne Task Force Commander.** If the forcible entry operation is an airborne assault, it will be delivered by airlift forces from either the CONUS, an ISB, or theater airbase. The airborne task force commander will normally organize the parachute assault force, airlift force, and follow-on airland forces in such a way as to best accomplish the mission based on the CONOPS. The command relationships established among the commander, airborne task force, the commander, airlift force, the JFACC, and other designated commanders of the forcible entry force is an important decision. An establishing JFC directive is essential to ensure unity of effort within and for the support of the airborne assault force. The airborne task force commander will normally exercise responsibility for the airlift plan, to include priority of airdrop and airland sorties, the preparatory fires plan, and the ground tactical plan in the airhead. The airborne task force commander's responsibilities end upon achievement of a secure airhead line and the establishment of either a JFLCC or designated ground commander command post in the airhead.

f. **Command and Control of Special Operations Forces.** When directed, Commander, US Special Operations Command, provides CONUS-based SOF to a GCC. The GCC normally exercises combatant command (command authority) of assigned and

Effective and efficient airspace management complements and supports the joint force commander's operational objectives.

operational control of attached SOF through the commander, theater special operations command (TSOC). When a GCC establishes and employs multiple JTFs and independent task forces (TFs) concurrently, the TSOC commander may establish and employ multiple joint special operations task forces to manage SOF assets and accommodate JTF/TF SO requirements. Accordingly, the GCC, as the common superior, normally will establish command relationships between the joint SO task force commanders and JTF/TF commanders. SOF liaison to the JFC is particularly important in order to coordinate operations of the supported/supporting SO force and advise the JFC of SOF capabilities and limitations. SOF liaison to the JFC is particularly important to coordinate operations of the supported/supporting SO force, advise the JFC of SOF capabilities and limitations, and to deconflict and synchronize SOF that may already be operating in the area. When conducting forcible entry operations into an area where SOF are already employed, it is imperative that both conventional and SO synchronize and coordinate their respective operations/missions.

g. **Forcible Entry Employing a Combination of Forces.** Forcible entry operations employing a combination of airborne, air assault, SOF, and AFs (to include multinational forces with these capabilities), **may be under the command of the JFC or a Service or functional component commander** and must be closely coordinated. The command relationships between the JFC and subordinate component commanders are critical to success of these operations. Once the forcible entry has been accomplished, follow-on or transition operations may require changes in command relationships to support the JFC's plan. Supporting operations will be coordinated with the supported commander.

h. **Command Relationships During Planning.** Forcible entry operations can have unique command relationships during the planning phase to ensure that air, land, maritime, space, and SO considerations are factored into decisions made concerning the conduct of the forcible entry operation.

5. **Airspace Control**

Airspace management increases combat effectiveness by promoting the safe, efficient, and flexible use of airspace with a minimum of restraint placed on airspace users—all while complementing and supporting the JFC's operational objectives. C2 of airspace requires two key elements: a control authority and a control system.

For further details on airspace control, refer to JP 3-52, Joint Airspace Control.

a. **Airspace Control Authority (ACA).** The JFC normally designates an ACA, who has overall responsibility for establishing and operating the airspace control system. The ACA monitors, assesses, and controls operational area airspace and directs changes in accordance with the JFC's intent.

(1) **Airspace Control Authority During Amphibious Operations.** JP 3-02, *Amphibious Operations*, and JP 3-52, *Joint Airspace Control*, provide detailed discussions on airspace control during amphibious assault operations.

(2) **Airspace Control Authority During Airborne/Air Assault Force Operations.** When an airborne/air assault force is the supported entry force in a forcible entry operation, the air component commander for the operation or JFACC (if designated) may use airborne C2 assets to enhance coordination and control of joint air operations and airspace management.

(a) The distances involved and the duration of airborne and air assault operations may require **establishing special air traffic control facilities or special tactics teams (STTs)** to extend detailed control into the objective area.

(b) The volume of air traffic throughout the airhead demands careful coordination to **limit potential conflict and to enable the success of mission-essential operations within the airhead.** A **high-density airspace control zone (HIDACZ)** may be established around a drop zone (DZ) or landing zone (LZ), which includes sufficient terrain and airspace to permit safe and efficient air traffic control. The HIDACZ can be nominated by the ground force commander and should, at a minimum, include the airspace bounded by the airhead line. Within the HIDACZ, **all aircraft flights should be coordinated with the DZ, LZ, and the agency responsible for controlling the joint airspace.** The air mission commander coordinates with the assault force commander to select the time on target and the direction of approach into and through the airhead.

b. **Airspace Control System.** The forces involved in the operation largely **determine the choices available to the ACA in designating an airspace control system** to control joint air operations; system interoperability will also be a major determining factor. For the airspace control system to function effectively, **the ACA must maximize and enhance the capabilities of the collective force using existing control systems.**

(1) **Airspace Control System During Amphibious Operations.** The airspace control system during amphibious operations is discussed in detail in JP 3-02, *Amphibious Operations.*

(2) **Airspace Control System During Airborne/Air Assault Force Operations.** The ACA will normally control the airspace through the **theater air control system (TACS)** and the **Army air-ground system (AAGS)** in forcible entries. Situations may limit establishment of ground systems and require airborne or seabased systems to conduct airspace control. Commanders and staffs should closely monitor and plan the employment of critical communication nodes within TACS/AAGS.

6. Air Defense Command and Control

The operational area, including ingress and egress routes, must be fully protected by an integrated air defense system consisting of air, land, maritime, and space assets supported by cyberspace capabilities. The joint force is particularly vulnerable to attacks by enemy aircraft or surface-to-surface missiles during the early stages of a forcible entry. **The primary objectives for air and missile defense operations are to assist in gaining air superiority and protecting the assault force. The area air defense commander (AADC) is responsible for integrating the joint force air defense effort.** All available surface-to-air assets should be incorporated into the overall air defense plan and comply with procedures and weapons control measures established by the AADC. **The AADC will exercise a degree of control of all systems** through established guidelines, determination of weapons control status, and JFC-approved procedural controls.

a. **Air Defense Command and Control During an Amphibious Assault.** The AADC bears overall responsibility for defensive counterair operations of the joint force. In amphibious operations, the AADC may divide the airspace into regions or sectors with regional air defense commanders (RADCs) or sector air defense commanders (SADCs) to enhance the decentralized execution of the defensive counterair operations. See JP 3-02, *Amphibious Operations*, for more information on air defense C2 in an amphibious assault. To understand the planning and execution of air defense during an amphibious raid or assault and how the maritime commanders and their staffs C2 these operations and function as an RADC or SADC, refer to JP 3-02, *Amphibious Operations*; JP 3-32, *Command and Control of Joint Maritime Operations*; and JP 3-01, *Countering Air and Missile Threats*.

b. **Air Defense Command and Control During Airborne/Air Assault**

(1) **During air movement to the operational area, the AADC will normally control air defense operations from an airborne platform** (e.g., Airborne Warning and Control System). In practice, extended distances from staging bases to designated operational areas may require the AADC to delegate control responsibilities to an air control

element on board the airborne platform. Initial air defense assets may be limited to fighter aircraft only. Control of these aircraft will normally be exercised through established procedural controls.

(2) **Forces initially entering the area of operations (AO) will be accompanied by organic short-range air defense systems** that must be integrated into the air defense C2 architecture. Planned procedural control measures and guidelines may be established by the AADC to expedite integration of assets.

(3) With force buildup and the introduction of follow-on forces into the lodgment area, **more robust high to medium altitude air defense systems will likely become available.** These systems must establish communications with the AADC's C2 agency and be incorporated into the established air defense system.

(4) Once established, **designated AADC control and reporting centers will normally assume air defense control responsibilities** for forces external to an established AOA or AO as defined by the JFC or the initiating directive.

(5) **Specific implications for forces supporting CAF are addressed below.**

(a) Participating naval aircraft may be placed under the control of the appropriate C2 agency.

(b) In some circumstances, naval air defense systems aboard participating ships may be limited. Accordingly, the AADC should take measures to ensure that a supporting AF is protected by other means.

7. Communications

Communications systems supporting forcible entry operations must be **interoperable, agile, trusted, and shared.** Interoperability can be achieved through commonality, compatibility, standardization, and liaison. To support agile forces and operational concepts, the communication architecture should be adaptable to a wide range of missions without the need for reconfiguration. The joint force must have confidence in the capabilities of the network and the validity of the information made available by the network. Agile connectivity and effective data exchange should incorporate internet protocol integration when possible. Sharing allows for the mutual use of information services or capabilities between entities in the operational area. Typical forcible entry operations communications will employ single and multichannel tactical satellites (TACSATs); commercial satellite communications (SATCOM); and single-channel ultrahigh frequency (UHF), very high frequency, and high frequency radios. The communications system directorate of a joint staff (J-6) is responsible for providing input to orders, plans, and coordinating communications system support and services during operations.

a. **Communications System Planning.** Once the JFC establishes the specific C2 organization for the forcible entry operation, the information exchange requirements are established as communications system planning begins. Communications system planning must be an integral part of joint force planning. The J-6 is responsible for planning and establishing the communications system and the communications estimate of supportability during course of action (COA) development and selection under the crisis action planning (CAP) process. Communications system planning must be conducted in close coordination with the intelligence directorate of a joint staff (J-2) to identify specialized equipment and dissemination requirements for some types of information. Because communications systems must be built-up at the objective area, some aspects of communications support are unique in forcible entry operations.

For further details on communications system planning, refer to JP 6-0, Joint Communications System.

b. **Communications Support for Amphibious Force Operations**. JP 3-02, *Amphibious Operations*, and appropriate Service doctrine and tactics, techniques, and procedures should be consulted for fundamental principles, considerations, and best practices related to communications support for an amphibious raid or assault.

c. **Communications Support for Airborne/Air Assault Force Operations.** Communications requirements vary with the mission, size, composition, geography, and location of the joint force and the senior headquarters. Significant considerations for airborne and air assault operations include the use of ISBs and **airborne C2 platforms, to include en route mission planning and intelligence sharing,** which can add to the complexity of managing the communications architecture. **Airborne/air assault forces will initially deploy with a limited communications capability,** largely based on UHF SATCOM. Communications support becomes more robust as signal units and equipment enter the operational area via airdrop or are air landed into the airhead.

(1) C2 relationships, nets, frequency assignments, codes, navigational aids, and any other communication issues **must be resolved before the assault phase begins.**

(2) **Long-range radio communications may be necessary** with US-based forces or ISBs to facilitate control of personnel, supplies, and equipment into the airhead or lodgment. **Long-range communications are initially established from higher to lower headquarters.** The primary means of long range communications will be satellite based. The higher headquarters may be on land, sea, or air and may maintain contact through retransmission and relay sites. The communications plan must ensure interoperability with the overall joint force communications architecture and provide the redundancy for CAF and subordinate commanders to adequately C2 operations.

(3) **Ground commanders in airlift aircraft may communicate with the chain of command over the Army secure en route communications package.** Normally, the airlift mission commander and the airborne task force commander are in the same aircraft.

The senior ground commander can advise embarked ground commanders of changes in the ground tactical situation or to the air movement plan.

(4) **Airborne/air assault forcible entry operations require the use of redundant airborne and ground command posts.** Normally, a joint force airborne command post will operate from a joint airborne communications center and command post, while a command post from the airborne/air assault force will operate from fixed-wing platform with required communications installed or a specially configured C2 rotary-wing aircraft.

(5) **TACSAT downlink** and **other en route communications systems** can be used to communicate with US Air Force STTs, air mobility liaison officers, contingency response elements, and contingency response teams in objective areas. The use of **special navigational aids** and **homing devices** to direct aircraft to specified areas (e.g., a designated DZ) may be necessary. Specialized airborne/air assault force personnel (e.g., STTs or long-range surveillance units) are equipped with **navigational aids**, **global positioning systems**, and **homing devices.** These teams will be employed early to guide the airborne/air assault forces, and provide reconnaissance, surveillance, visual flight rules service, and limited instrument flight rules air traffic control service. Other joint force assets such as SOF or Marine force reconnaissance elements are also capable of performing some of these functions.

8. Rules of Engagement

a. The rules of engagement (ROE) are developed by the Joint Staff and CCDRs and reviewed and approved by the President and Secretary of Defense (SecDef) or other authorized military authority for promulgation and dissemination. ROE ensure actions, especially force employment, are consistent with military objectives, domestic and international law, and national policy. Joint forces operate in accordance with applicable ROE, conduct warfare in compliance with US and international laws, and fight within restraints and constraints specified by their commanders. Properly developed ROE must be clear, tailored to the situation, reviewed for legal sufficiency, and included in training. ROE typically will vary from operation to operation and may change during an operation. The challenge for a JFC is to ensure that the ROE for a forcible entry operation **provides the commander with the flexibility to accomplish the mission, while assuring adherence to political, legal, operational, and diplomatic factors the force may encounter.** The ROE also provides a specified level of protection to those persons and/or objects entitled to protected status.

For additional information on ROE, see Chairman of the Joint Chiefs of Staff Instruction (CJCSI) 3121.01B, Standing Rules of Engagement/Standing Rules for the Use of Force for US Forces.

b. Forcible entry operations are normally characterized by a high operational tempo and violent execution. Circumstances may require unexpected changes to ROE. Commanders must be attuned to changes in the tactical and political situations, specifically as they relate to ROE, and ensure that members of their force receive **timely notification of ROE changes.**

c. To mitigate unnecessary loss of life and unintended collateral damage, commanders should ensure that members of their force are adequately trained in the application of force from nonlethal to lethal.

9. Friendly Fire Prevention

a. The complexity of forcible entry operations increases the potential for friendly fire incidents and demands **efforts by all elements of the joint force to deliberately reduce the risk of friendly fire.** Friendly force tracking provides JFCs with enhanced situational awareness that can help to reduce friendly fire.

b. **Primary Mechanisms for Friendly Fire Prevention.** Detailed integration of maneuver, fire support, and air and missile defense operations are required to prevent friendly fire incidents. Coordination center personnel seek to prevent friendly fire through close coordination at all levels by maintaining situational awareness. Use of FSCMs, coordination of position areas, and the consideration of the locations of friendly forces during target analysis all contribute to safeguarding friendly units.

For further details on preventing friendly fire, refer to JP 3-01, Countering Air and Missile Threats; *JP 3-09,* Joint Fire Support; *JP 3-09.3,* Close Air Support; *and JP 3-52,* Joint Airspace Control.

c. **Liaison.** Liaison elements provided by supporting components can advise supported commanders on component capabilities and limitations, and can assist in the coordination, integration and synchronization of operations, ultimately preventing losses from friendly fire.

Intentionally Blank

CHAPTER III
PLANNING

"Now the general who wins a battle makes many calculations in his temple before the battle is fought. The general who loses a battle makes but few calculations before-hand. Thus do many calculations lead to victory, and few calculations to defeat: How much more no calculation at all! It is by attention to this point that I can see who is likely to win or lose."

Sun Tzu,
The Art of War, c. 500 BC

1. Purpose

This chapter provides information on planning forcible entry operations. Existing joint planning processes and considerations are used in planning these operations.

2. Forcible Entry and the Joint Planning Process

Joint planning is conducted using a disciplined process described in policies and procedures established in the **Joint Operation Planning and Execution System (JOPES), JOPP** (see Figure III-1). These processes facilitate both deliberate planning and CAP. During deliberate planning, the operation plan (OPLAN) or concept plan (CONPLAN), and supporting annexes, for an operation or campaign are prepared. This includes forcible entry operation requirements. CAP is used to expand an approved or directed COA into a detailed operation order (OPORD) and sourced time-phased force and deployment data, by

The Joint Operation Planning Process

Step 1	Planning Initiation
Step 2	Mission Analysis
Step 3	Course of Action (COA) Development
Step 4	COA Analysis and Wargaming
Step 5	COA Comparison
Step 6	COA Approval
Step 7	Plan or Order Development

Figure III-1. The Joint Operation Planning Process

modifying an existing OPLAN, expanding an existing CONPLAN, or developing a completely new OPORD when there is no preexisting OPLAN.

 a. Forcible entry operations require extensive JIPOE. The primary purpose of JIPOE is to support the JFC's planning and decision making by identifying, analyzing, and estimating the enemy's centers of gravity, critical factors, capabilities, limitations, requirements, vulnerabilities, intentions, and COAs that are most likely to be encountered by the entry force.

 b. Time, distance, physical attributes of the operational area, agreement/arrangement with other host nations, or the nature of the crisis may dictate the deployment of a joint force to staging areas outside the US. Likewise, authorizations may be required to conduct advance force operations in the operational area to prepare the operational environment for the introduction of combat forces. Commanders and operational planners may have to compress planning timelines to meet time-sensitive mission requirements. **Time-sensitive situations will likely demand:** establishing joint staffs and exchanging liaison personnel as soon as command relationships are defined; conducting parallel planning at all command levels; establishing the supporting intelligence architecture from national to tactical levels; pre-positioning airlift and sealift with supported units; loading unit sets of equipment on surge sealift ships at US or allied seaports of embarkation (SPOEs); directing the movement of sea-based pre-positioned equipment to the operational area; embarking personnel and equipment at US or allied aerial ports of embarkation (APOEs); careful planning for aerial and amphibious embarkation and debarkation; and conducting reconnaissance and surveillance operations.

For further detail on amphibious embarkation and debarkation, see JP 3-02.1, Amphibious Embarkation and Debarkation.

 c. Forcible entry will require well-trained and well-prepared joint forces capable of executing operations on short-notice. It is essential that all key elements associated with the operation are included in the planning forum from the onset. This ensures resources needed are available in a timely manner and that ample time is available for preparation. When operations require specialists, it is essential that the requirements are identified early and those organizations are included in planning.

3. Forcible Entry Planning Considerations

 JOPP underpins planning at all levels and for missions across the range of military operations. The process is designed to facilitate interaction between commander, staff, and subordinate headquarters throughout planning. Often forcible entry planning occurs within CAP. The JFC, staff, and subordinate and/or supporting commanders and staffs follow JOPP and consider the following factors when developing forcible entry operations.

 a. **Planning Initiation.** The President, SecDef, or the Chairman of the Joint Chiefs of Staff may initiate planning for forcible entry operations to develop military options to respond to a potential or actual crisis. Additionally, GCCs and other commanders may initiate planning on their own authority when they identify a planning requirement not directed by higher authority.

b. **Mission Analysis.** The joint force mission describes the essential task or set of tasks, together with the purpose, clearly indicating the action to be taken and the reason for doing so. In analyzing a forcible entry operation, the JFC and staff consider:

(1) Higher mission and guidance.

(2) A thorough JIPOE, including:

(a) Threat to joint forces en route to, and operating in, the operational area.

(b) Geography of the operational area.

(c) Lodgment terrain and infrastructure, with a critical eye on the ability to support follow-on operations.

(d) An understanding of the information environment.

(3) Operational reach and approach.

(4) Forces available including multinational and indigenous.

(5) Time available.

(6) Strategic and operational aims, including the military end state.

(7) Command relationships and force composition.

(8) Combat power required to achieve operational objectives.

(9) Operational restrictions that may inhibit subordinate commanders.

(10) Initial staff estimates.

(11) Media and public perception.

(12) Political environment.

For more discussion on staff estimates, see JP 5-0, Joint Operation Planning.

c. **Course Of Action Development.** In the development of a forcible entry COA, five phases are addressed: preparation and deployment, assault, stabilization of the lodgment, introduction of follow-on forces, and termination or transition. To produce a valid COA, the following should be considered (Chapter IV, "Operations," further expands on the five phases):

(1) **Phase I (Preparation and Deployment).** Considerations include the following:

(a) Determine the forcible entry option(s) to be executed, how those operations will support campaign success, and the command relationships required.

(b) Determine deployment sequencing of forces that supports gaining access into the objective area, the initial assault, reinforcement, and the introduction of follow-on forces.

(c) Determine requirements for local air and maritime superiority to conduct the forcible entry operation.

(d) Determine forcible entry go/no-go criteria.

(e) Determine logistic factors and establishing airhead and beachhead resupply responsibilities.

(f) Determine feasibility of clandestine insertion of strategic surveillance assets prior to commencement of the assault.

(2) **Phase II (Assault).** Considerations include the following:

(a) Analyzing objectives and potential lodgment with regard to:

1. The proposed ground tactical plan.

2. Potential capability for air and sea landing of personnel and equipment.

3. Space within the lodgment and maneuver space for future operations.

4. Vulnerability to interdiction and counterattacks.

(b) Operating facilities and/or infrastructure to support operations.

(c) Identify forces securing airheads and/or beachheads (e.g., advance, pre-assault, and LFs).

(d) Reception of reinforcing forces (if required) and follow-on forces for subsequent operations.

(3) **Phase III (Stabilization of the Lodgment).** Considerations include the following:

(a) Identify the requirements for reinforcing forces and projected deployment flow, with attention to:

1. Cross-loading among lift assets.

2. Task-organized by arrival sequence.

(b) Identify potential restrictions and/or limitations in force flow, and eliminating and/or reducing accordingly.

(c) Establish redundancy of force capability in deployment flow for added flexibility.

(d) Establish call-forward procedures for reinforcing forces, if required.

(e) Calculate throughput capability of ports of debarkation.

(f) Determine preparation requirements needed to reinforce forces for combat on arrival.

(g) Determine requirements for expansion of the lodgment.

(h) Establish force link-up procedures.

(4) **Phase IV (Introduction of Follow-on Forces).** Considerations include the following:

(a) Identifying tasks for follow-on forces.

(b) Preparing for arrival of follow-on forces.

(c) Coordinating arrival and/or disposition of any allocated maritime pre-positioning force (MPF) and Army pre-positioned stocks (APS).

(d) Throughput capacity of ports of debarkation.

(5) **Phase V (Termination or Transition).** Considerations include the following:

(a) Continuing planning and coordination actions initiated in early phases.

(b) Planning for reconstitution and redeployment of the assault force.

(c) Planning to terminate the forcible entry portion of the joint operation.

(d) Planning for transition to follow-on operations or termination of the entire joint operation. Planning for follow-on operations may include the use of nonlethal weapons to limit casualties, collateral damage, and reconstruction requirements.

(e) Planning for hand over to civil authorities (if applicable).

JP 3-57, Civil-Military Operations, *provides guidance on transition planning.*

d. **Course Of Action Analysis and Wargaming.** The commander and staff will analyze each COA separately according to the commander's guidance to bring out relevant factors in each COA. Wargaming provides the means for the commander and participants to analyze a COA and obtain insights not otherwise discernable.

e. **Course Of Action Comparison.** The staff will evaluate COAs using governing factors identified during the wargame in order to identify the COA with the highest probability of success.

f. **Course Of Action Approval.** The staff determines the best COA and presents a recommendation to the commander for approval.

g. **Plan or Order Development.** Deliberate planning results in plan development, while CAP typically will lead directly to OPORD development.

JP 5-0, Joint Operation Planning, *provides guidance regarding JOPES and JOPP.*

CHAPTER IV
OPERATIONS

"Success in war depends upon the Golden Rule of War. Speed—Simplicity—Boldness."

General George S. Patton, US Army
Inscribed in his field notebook - 1921

1. Purpose

This chapter provides information on the execution of forcible entry operations. Section A, "Integration and Synchronization," describes the five phases of a forcible entry operation and discusses the integration and synchronization of these operations in the context of the forcible entry phases. Section B, "Supporting Operations," focuses on supporting operations such as intelligence, IO, and SO in support of forcible entry operations.

SECTION A. INTEGRATION AND SYNCHRONIZATION

2. Introduction

a. **General.** This section highlights some common issues and considerations that integrate and synchronize activities during a forcible entry operation. The discussion that follows is not a checklist, but may be used by JFCs and staffs as appropriate to meet their specific needs.

b. **Rehearsals.** In order to integrate, synchronize, and confirm the timing of an operation, **the JFC may choose to** conduct a rehearsal (other benefits of rehearsals are listed in Figure IV-1). Rehearsals at the operational level range in scope from **joint force exercises** (driven by resource, time, space, and force availability constraints), to **command post exercises** supported by computer aided-simulations, to **commanders and/or key personnel conferences**. The decision to conduct rehearsals will be influenced by the time available and by OPSEC considerations.

Operation Plan Rehearsal Benefits

- Common Understanding
- Unity of Effort
- Articulate Supporting Intents
- Subordinate and Supporting Commanders' Questions
- Branches or Sequels
- Integration and Synchronization

Figure IV-1. Operation Plan Rehearsal Benefits

3. Forcible Entry Operations Phases

Forcible entry operations are normally conducted during the "seize the initiative" or "dominate" phase of a joint operation. Within the context of these phases established by a higher-level JFC, the forcible entry operation commander may establish additional phases that fit the forcible entry CONOPS. **Forcible entry operations may be planned and executed in the five phases listed in Figure IV-2.** Planning for each phase should include branch and sequel planning. Transitions between these phases are designed to be distinct shifts in focus by the joint force, often accompanied by changes in command or support relationships. The activities that predominate during a given phase, however, rarely align with neatly definable breakpoints. The need to move into another phase normally is identified by assessing that a set of objectives are achieved or that the enemy has acted in a manner that requires a major change in focus for the joint force and is therefore usually event driven, not time driven. Changing the focus of the operation takes time and may require changing commander's objectives, desired effects, measures of effectiveness, priorities, command relationships, force allocation, or even the organization of the operational area.

For further information on phasing in joint operations, refer to JP 3-0, Joint Operations, *and JP 5-0,* Joint Operation Planning.

a. **Preparation and Deployment (Phase I).** Forcible entry operations are conducted by organizations whose force structures permit rapid deployment into the objective area. Joint forces may deploy directly to the operational area or to staging areas to prepare for subsequent operations.

(1) **Planning. The JFC, the component commanders, and their staffs must be intimately involved in planning and executing the deployment of forces to the operational area.** Planning must begin as early as possible, including developing contingencies during peacetime. Staffs should plan all phases, including transition. During this phase, planners should include multinational partners, other DOD agencies, US

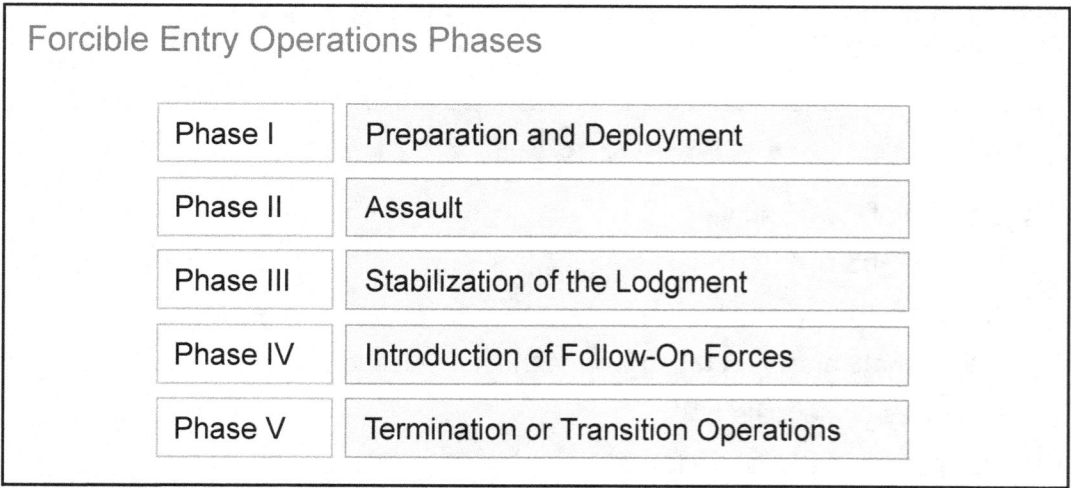

Forcible Entry Operations Phases	
Phase I	Preparation and Deployment
Phase II	Assault
Phase III	Stabilization of the Lodgment
Phase IV	Introduction of Follow-On Forces
Phase V	Termination or Transition Operations

Figure IV-2. Forcible Entry Operations Phases

Government departments and agencies, and interagency participants based on the design for the operation or campaign and OPSEC restrictions.

(2) **Movement.** Forcible entry operations involve **movement planning** from both strategic and operational perspectives. These operations involve movement from marshalling areas as well as loading and departure from ports and ISBs for the sequenced movement of forces to objective area(s) in accordance with the OPORD. During this phase, the forcible entry force will typically conduct **rehearsals of the operation** as time and resources permit.

(3) **Joint Intelligence Preparation of the Operational Environment. Increased intelligence collection efforts** focus on gathering information to satisfy priority intelligence requirements that the JFC requires and determining if the required conditions for the assault have been established (e.g., local air superiority has been achieved). **Reconnaissance and surveillance assets** (e.g., SOF) **may be inserted into the objective area** during this phase as part of this effort.

(4) **Transition to Assault.** During phase I, **the joint force sets the conditions that are required for a successful assault** by isolating the lodgment and achieving local air and maritime. Air interdiction, naval surface fire support (NSFS), SOF missions, CO, and/or other actions to prepare assault objectives will normally occur prior to the commitment of assault forces. In other situations, political or operational considerations may preclude such actions prior to the initiation of the assault phase of the operation.

(5) **Insertion of Special Operations Force.** In addition to conducting SO during the assault, SOF may be introduced to the area well in advance of a possible assault to develop or prepare an area for forcible entry. For example, UW and the use of surrogate forces can significantly reduce enemy defensive capabilities. Special reconnaissance may provide detailed intelligence not available by any other means. SO can be vital to shaping or deterrence actions throughout the period preceding the forcible entry. SOF regional expertise and support to JIPOE are often vital in planning and execution.

b. **Assault (Phase II).** Phase II begins with **joint force assaults** to seize initial objectives in the lodgment and concludes with the **consolidation of those objectives.**

(1) **Initial Assaults. Initial assaults are designed to surprise and overwhelm the enemy with decisive force and to protect assault forces** as they accomplish assigned missions. **SOF and information related capabilities may be employed** in advance of assault forces to identify, clarify, and modify conditions in the operational area; and/or to conduct reconnaissance, surveillance, and interdiction operations well beyond the initial assault objectives. Opening entry points will involve actual assault by various combinations of amphibious and airborne forces to achieve a coup de main or enable follow-on operations through the seizure of existing ports and airfields or the establishment of expeditionary facilities. SOF may be used in combination with naval forces to conduct assaults to open entry points. **Planning for this phase may include pre-assault strikes** by cruise missiles, armed unmanned aircraft, fixed-wing aircraft, attack helicopters, and/or NSFS to destroy

enemy forces in the objective areas and/or enemy ground force reserves, aircraft, theater missiles, weapons of mass destruction (WMD), and naval forces that could disrupt the operation. Assault forces may use multiple approaches and entry points to deceive the adversary and diminish his ability to observe, orient, decide, and act.

(2) **Overcoming Obstacles.** The JFC will be faced with natural and man-made obstacles intended to restrict or halt movement that allows the enemy to mass its forces and repel the assault. Naval mine countermeasures (MCM) forces may be required to conduct MCM operations in order to clear transit and assault lanes of sea-based mines and/or obstacles in order to facilitate rapid movement of LFs and follow-on forces from the sea. Explosive ordnance disposal personnel and combat engineers enhance the mobility of assault forces on land by clearing roads and airfields of explosive hazards, mines, improvised explosive devices, and other obstacles; and by conducting forward aviation combat engineering operations.

MINES AT WONSAN—KOREA, 1950

During the rapid advance following the Inchon landing and breakout from Pusan, US and ROK [Republic of Korea] forces advanced rapidly up the eastern coast. The US X Corps planned for an amphibious assault at Wonsan, the only useable North Korean landing area.

Evidence began to mount that the North Koreans were mining the coastal waters of North Korea. Three US ships, the Brush, Mansfield, and Magpie, struck mines and suffered heavy damage. Although intelligence sources indicated enemy mines were being laid in coastal waters, little was known about the location and extent of these mine fields. North Korean interests certainly dictated, however, that the sea approaches to Wonsan should be mined.

In a series of conferences from 2 to 4 October, Admiral Struble and his staff decided to form the Advance Force JTF [Joint Task Force] 7, which would proceed to the objective area and begin minesweeping at the earliest possible date. All minesweepers available were to be concentrated for the task. The group comprised 21 vessels, including 10 American and 8 Japanese minesweepers, and 1 South Korean vessel used as a minesweeper. Minesweeping operations at Wonsan began on 10 October. A search by helicopter over the harbor channel showed it to be heavily mined inside the 30-fathom curve. The plan to sweep this channel was canceled and another substituted-to sweep from the 100-fathom curve down the Russian Hydropac Channel passing between Yodo and Hwangt'o-do Islands. By 12 October this channel had been swept a distance of twenty-four miles from the 100-fathom curve. Ten miles remained to the inner harbor.

At this point the novel idea was advanced of exploding mines along a narrow passageway by aerial bombing which would permit the lead

---

sweeps to pass. On 12 October thirty-nine planes from the carriers Philippine Sea and Leyte flew down the Russian channel dropping 1,000-pound bombs.

Three minesweepers, the Pirate, Pledge, and Incredible, then entered the bombed channel to resume minesweeping. Northwest of Yo-do Island the Pirate struck a mine at 1209; the Pledge hit one six minutes later. Both vessels sank. As the Incredible, third in line, maneuvered into safe water, enemy shore batteries opened fire. Twelve men went down with the two sunken ships. One enlisted man died later from wounds. At least 33 others were wounded and injured in varying degrees; some sources place the number of wounded as high as 99. The Incredible itself rescued 27 survivors.

The menace of shore batteries was removed on 17 October when ground forces of the ROK I Corps, which had already captured Wonsan, gained control of the peninsulas and islands commanding the harbor approaches.

Casualties from mines continued. On 18 October two ROK Navy vessels struck mines in the Wonsan area; one was disabled at the entrance to the harbor, and the other, a minesweeper, was sunk. The next day a Japanese minesweeper struck a mine and sank. The risk of sending transports with troops to the beaches was still great. The presence of ground mines in the shallow water made necessary a thorough magnetic sweep of the close-in approaches to the landing beaches. Because troops of the ROK I Corps were now well past Wonsan, the military situation did not warrant an unnecessary risk in unloading the Marine units. Admiral Struble, therefore, recommended that they not be unloaded on 20 October as planned, but that D-day be deferred until the minesweeping could be completed. Admiral Joy and General MacArthur concurred.

South to the Naktong, North to the Yalu
Roy E. Appleman - 1961

(3) **Main Assault.** Assault forces will enter objective areas via parachute assault, air LFs, helicopter-borne air assault, and amphibious assault or raid. Throughout the assault phase, **landed forces must have immediately available joint fire support** to destroy, interdict, or suppress enemy forces and missile defense. The joint force must maintain the initiative and rapidly prepare to receive follow-on forces to develop the combat power necessary to secure the lodgment. CAS and NSFS are critical resources during the assault. Depending on resources available to the JFC, **the introduction of LFs may be combined with simultaneous strikes against other key enemy assets** throughout the operational area in order to prevent the enemy's ability to react effectively.

(4) **Transition to Stabilizing the Lodgment.** The assault may be capped by offensive, defensive, or retrograde operations as described by the JFC's operational concept,

and by the introduction of follow-on forces to assist in securing the lodgment and continue on to follow-on operations without an operational pause.

c. **Stabilization of the Lodgment (Phase III).** Stabilization involves **securing the lodgment** to protect the force and ensure the continuous landing of personnel and materiel, **organizing the lodgment** to support the increasing flow of forces and logistic resource requirements, and **expanding the lodgment** as required to support the joint force in preparing for and executing follow-on operations. Force buildup begins with the securing of objectives by assault forces and must be consistent with the overall operation or campaign plan with regard to the proper balance of combat forces and logistics required to conduct subsequent operations. The joint force takes immediate steps to optimize lodgment throughput capabilities.

(1) **Securing the Lodgment.** Whether the forcible entry is envisioned as the establishment of a lodgment to enable future combat operations, or as a coup de main, the lodgment must be secured and protected in order for it to serve as an entry point for follow-on forces and sustainment. Based on the JFC's analysis of the threat and available forces, the lodgment is expanded as required. Lodgment security is continuous and enables organization and expansion.

(2) **Organizing the Lodgment.** Details concerning the introduction of follow-on forces must be prepared during the planning phase of the operation. Commanders introduce reinforcing forces as required based on the tactical situation. All means of delivery are exploited to maximize combat power in the lodgment. Aerial ports of debarkation (APODs) and seaports of debarkation (SPODs) must be secured and repaired as necessary.

The joint force must maintain the initiative and rapidly prepare to receive follow-on forces to develop the combat power necessary to secure the lodgment.

Appropriate logistic and communications infrastructure must be established as quickly as possible to facilitate the reception of follow-on forces.

(3) **Expanding the Lodgment.** Expansion is when the lodgment is not fully established and the introduction of combat power significantly contributes to the development of the security situation. During the expansion, the capacity of ground forces to maintain the lodgment in the face of a coherent enemy response should significantly increase.

(4) **Transition to Introducing Follow-on Forces.** Though intended to conduct follow-on operations, in extreme circumstances, **follow-on forces may be required to assist assault forces in the seizure of initial objectives,** or may be used to help secure and defend the lodgment. Provisions must be made to clear follow-on supplies and equipment immediately from offload points to maximize airlift and sealift efficiency. **The joint force must avoid an unnecessary operational pause.** The tempo of operations directed against the enemy must be maintained to prevent the enemy from reorganizing and effectively countering the establishment of the lodgment.

d. **Introduction of Follow-on Forces (Phase IV)**

(1) **Purpose of Follow-on Forces.** *(Note: This phase is required when subsequent operations are planned for conduct in or from the lodgment.)* Follow-on forces provide the JFC with **increased flexibility to conduct operations as required by operational conditions;** once the lodgment has been established with APODs and SPODs, a joint security area may be identified and developed to facilitate and provide security for subsequent support operations. Follow-on forces and equipment may flow via air LOCs and SLOCs into the APODs and SPODs located within the now-established lodgment. During this phase, joint logistics over-the-shore (JLOTS) operations commence in earnest. Follow-on forces may also deploy to the operational area to link up with pre-positioned equipment. Initially, airfield operations may be conducted in a combat environment. Airfield operations and security should conform to currently published guidance and in accordance with any valid intra-service agreements or plans. Once the airfield is secure and open for full operations, improvements can be made to provide the capacity for aircraft maintenance and parking. Follow-on force equipment will largely flow from pre-positioned stocks.

(2) **Ground Offensive Operations.** In some operations and campaigns, the follow-on forces will conduct ground offensive operations to link up with forces in the lodgment. This may involve offensive operations conducted by forces from the lodgment in conjunction with the attacks being conducted by friendly forces beyond the lodgment. At Anzio, in 1944, reinforced Allied forces succeeded in breaking out of the lodgment and linking up with the US Fifth Army as part of a larger offensive across the Italian peninsula.

Elements of a Marine expeditionary unit move from ship-to-shore by way of landing craft, air cushion

(3) **Maritime Pre-Positioned Force and Army Pre-Positioned Stocks Employment.** MPF and APS options provide the JFC with **significant combat capabilities to initiate or prosecute follow-on operations.** Fundamental requirements for MPF or APS operations include intertheater lift and a secure environment (e.g., arrival airfields, ports, and/or beaches) for arrival, off-load, and assembly of forces. These are the conditions that will be achieved during the stabilization phase of a forcible entry operation.

(a) **Maritime Pre-Positioned Force.** The purpose of an MPF operation is to rapidly establish a Marine air-ground task force ashore that is prepared to conduct military operations.

(b) **Army Pre-Positioned Stocks.** When available, provides the GCC or designated subordinate JFC with a similarly responsive brigade size armored force to be employed rapidly in response to a crisis situation. Like the MPF, this capability consists of the equipment required by brigade combat teams (BCTs) and enabling units to conduct a wide range of operations.

(4) **Follow-on Force Preparation for Subsequent Operations.** Ideally, all follow-on forces will be organized and tailored so they are ready for combat upon arrival in the lodgment; however, in most situations, follow-on forces will require a period of time to link up with equipment, organize, and prepare for operations that follow the forcible entry. The following organizations can enable the start of subsequent operations.

(a) **Contingency Response Group.** The contingency response group (CRG) is composed of Air Force personnel and assets, trained and equipped to secure after seizure, assess, open, and initially operate airfields. The CRG provides engineer, security, communications, and airfield support assets needed to support the forcible entry effort. Special capabilities, not present in every CRG, include airborne, air assault, and pathfinder; expanded combat communications; and RED HORSE [Rapid Engineer Deployable Heavy Operational Repair Squadron Engineer] and/or expeditionary engineering.

(b) **Combat Communications Groups.** Air Force combat communications groups (CCGs) provide communications and air traffic control personnel/services, to include various deployable air traffic control and landing systems such as mobile control towers, tactical air navigation systems, and precision radar approach systems required to support all-weather aircraft operations. CCGs can also be deployed to temporarily restore damaged, destroyed, or incapacitated fixed resources during peacetime operations, and can deploy as an entire airfield package or may be tailored to provide the required level of air traffic control service. CCGs are organized to support DOD requirements as well as certain tactical communications projects. All packages contain an organic maintenance capability.

(c) **Air and Space Expeditionary Task Force Force Module.** This is an open-the-airfield Air Force module that contains the capabilities to open an airfield regardless of the follow-on mission or aircraft type. This module is representative of the baseline capability set and skill set, and the equipment is similar to the CRG. If planning time is available, this module is the preferred module for open-the-airfield forces.

(d) **Special Tactics Team .** STTs are comprised of Air Force combat control, combat weather, and pararescue personnel. The STT has the capability to assess, establish, and control LZs; to provide weather observations and forecasting; and to provide battlefield trauma care. They employ with airfield seizure forces, CRG, or unilaterally to provide terminal control of the airfield. Combat control personnel are qualified as joint terminal attack controllers.

(e) **820th Security Forces Group.** This Air Force unit can provide fully integrated, highly capable, force protection and contingency response forces for expeditionary airfield opening. The unit is capable of airborne insertion operations for 14-30 days and has the organic capability to provide airfield security and initial airfield assessment. The unit can link with initial entry/base seizure forces and provide a smooth transition to airfield opening forces

(f) **Air Force Special Tactics Teams and Tactical Air Control Party.** Air Force STT and tactics teams and tactical air control party performs both airspace and ground control for aircraft supporting the lodgment.

(g) **Maneuver Enhancement Brigade.** This Army brigade provides protection and enhances the mobility of supported forcible entry forces. Following a forcible entry assault the brigade supports BCTs with tailored engineer, military police,

CBRN, and other supporting capabilities required for successful subsequent entry and decisive operations.

e. **Termination or Transition Operations (Phase V).** The transition from a forcible entry operation to subsequent operations or termination must be an integral part of the planning phase of the joint deployment process. **A successful forcible entry operation is completed in one of two ways:** attainment of the campaign objectives (termination); or completion of the operational objectives wherein a lodgment is established for follow-on combat operations (transition).

(1) **Achievement of Operation or Campaign Objectives.** If the forcible entry operation accomplishes the strategic objectives, then the JFC may be directed to **reconstitute and redeploy the joint force** either to home station or to some other theater of operations.

(2) **Achievement of Operational Objectives.** In many cases, a forcible entry operation will probably be only one phase of a campaign or major operation. As such, **the forcible entry operation establishes the conditions for follow-on operations.** Follow-on forces generally focus on executing sequels to the forcible entry operation that are designed to achieve additional campaign objectives. These sequels include the full range of military operations across the operational phases depicted in JP 3-0, *Joint Operations*, (e.g., seize the initiative, dominate, or stabilize phases) as part of the larger operation.

For further details on stability operations, refer to JP 3-0, Joint Operations, *and JP 3-57,* Civil-Military Operations. *For further details on interagency coordination, refer to JP 3-08,* Interorganizational Coordination During Joint Operations.

For additional information regarding transition, refer to Department of Defense Instruction 3000.05, Stability Operations.

4. Integration and/or Synchronization Considerations

The following discussion illustrates the **type of activities that may occur at the JFC level** to integrate and synchronize a forcible entry operation. This list is not all-inclusive, but presents **activities for JFCs and staffs to consider** when synchronizing a typical forcible entry operation. The number and types of phases for forcible entry operations, as with all operations, may vary. As phasing is a key synchronization action, these activities are organized into the five phases of forcible entry operation presented earlier in this chapter. The example assumes that a combination of forcible entry capabilities will be used to obtain a lodgment as the initial operation of a larger campaign. These phases are normally sequential but may overlap. During planning, commanders must establish conditions for transitioning from one phase to another. The commander adjusts the phases to exploit opportunities presented by the enemy or to react to unforeseen situations.

a. **Phase I: Preparation and Deployment**

(1) An accurate time-phased force and deployment list (TPFDL) is developed up through level 4 detail.

(2) The JFC assigns complementary and/or deconflicted missions to components.

(3) Operational areas are designated.

(4) Command relationships are delineated.

(5) Rehearsals are conducted.

(6) The intelligence effort for components is prioritized.

(7) Initial air apportionment decisions are made.

(8) Targeting guidance is disseminated.

(9) Desired arrival sequence of forces in the operational area is matched to available transportation and validated with the time phased force and deployment data.

(10) Integration and/or synchronization with other (if any) operations is completed.

(11) Plan for the use and integration of the military activities that support strategic communication themes and messages—IO, PA, and defense support to public diplomacy (DSPD).

(12) Deception operations are executed.

(13) Advance force operations (e.g., countermine, air superiority, space superiority, cyberspace superiority, preparation of the operational environment, and isolation) to include SOF conducting required SOF core operations and activities which may include UW operations.

(14) Sustainment activities and/or requirements are planned.

(15) Plan for casualty operations is formulated.

(16) Fire support coordination and airspace coordinating measures are formulated.

(17) Surveillance assets in the assault areas are positioned and reporting.

b. **Phase II: Assault**

(1) Air apportionment is reassessed and revised.

(2) H-hour [specific time an operation or exercise begins] synchronization is completed among components.

(3) Modifications to existing plans and branches and/or sequels are deconflicted.

(4) Operational areas are activated.

(5) Fire support coordination and airspace coordinating measures are activated.

(6) Pre H-hour activities and/or staging are completed.

(7) Supported and supporting relationships among components are modified, as required.

(8) Provide for casualty evacuation.

(9) Link up with assault follow-on echelon and/or SOF.

c. **Phase III: Stabilization of the Lodgment**

(1) Terrain management issues are addressed.

(2) Clear airfield of unexploded explosive ordnance prior to any repair, maintenance, or operations.

(3) Runways, aprons, taxiways, and parking areas are repaired and maintained to support continuous air landed operations.

(4) Airspace management is coordinated.

(5) Medical evacuation is provided.

(6) TPFDL flow is managed.

d. **Phase IV: Introduction of Follow-on Forces**

(1) Force sequencing is continuously adjusted.

(2) Battle handover is completed.

(3) Reconstitution and/or redeployment of assault forces (e.g., embark the LF for a subsequent mission) is completed.

(4) Joint security operations issues are addressed.

(5) AOA is dissolved.

(6) Ports of debarkation are maintained to maximize and sustain throughput for follow-on forces.

e. **Phase V: Termination or Transition Operations**

(1) Joint force and/or component missions and command relationships are reorganized.

(2) Priorities of support are shifted.

(3) Transition to further operations in the "seize the initiative," "dominate," or "stabilize" phase of the joint operation.

SECTION B. SUPPORTING OPERATIONS

5. Special Operations Forces

SO are an integral part of forcible entry operations and these actions and operations are integrated to complement the achievement of strategic and operational objectives. SOF may be employed prior to forcible entry operations to collect intelligence, seize key terrain, organize and train guerrilla forces, and conduct other activities that facilitate the introduction of conventional forces. In the execution stages of a forcible entry operation, SOF can seize objectives, interdict targets (especially those that can severely disrupt the assault to open entry points), and conduct other operations to support the main force. In the closing stages

---

**MILITARY DECEPTION OPERATIONS
UTILIZING SPECIAL OPERATIONS FORCES DURING DESERT
STORM—IRAQ, 1991**

From 29 January until 16 February 1991, Naval Special Warfare Task Group elements conducted near-shore and off-shore reconnaissance missions in support of US Central Command's deception strategy to fix Iraqi attention on a potential amphibious assault by US Marines. The special reconnaissance missions resulted in the collection of information, established a naval presence along the Kuwaiti coast, and focused the attention of the Iraqi command on a possible maritime invasion. The deception effort culminated in a large-scale operation on the night of 23-24 February 1991, the eve of the ground offensive, which simulated a beach reconnaissance and clearing operation. The deception campaign prevented Iraqi units at the beaches from reinforcing those being attacked in the west.

SOURCE: United States Special Operations
Command History, 2nd Edition

---

of the operation, SOF can play a key role in transition or termination by working with host nation, multinational, interagency, and intergovernmental partners.

See JP 3-05, Special Operations, *for more information on SOF.*

6. Fires

In forcible entry operations, the initial assault forces are building combat power in the operational area from nothing as quickly as possible. They will normally have very minimal or no artillery support available for fire support in the early stages of the operation. Fires from aircraft (manned and unmanned) and/or naval platforms (surface/subsurface) take on added importance to compensate for the lack of artillery. The supported commander establishes the priority, timing, and effects of all fires within the boundaries of the designated operational area.

JP 3-09, Joint Fire Support, *and JP 3-02,* Amphibious Operations, *provide more information on fire support.*

7. Intelligence Support and Considerations

a. The JFC uses intelligence to decide what, why, when, where, and how to attack; determine forcible entry capabilities needed and task organization required to seize initial objective(s); support targeting and combat assessment; and anticipate future operations (see Figure IV-3). Counterintelligence (CI) helps the JFC maintain the element of surprise essential to forcible entry operations by supporting OPSEC and deception.

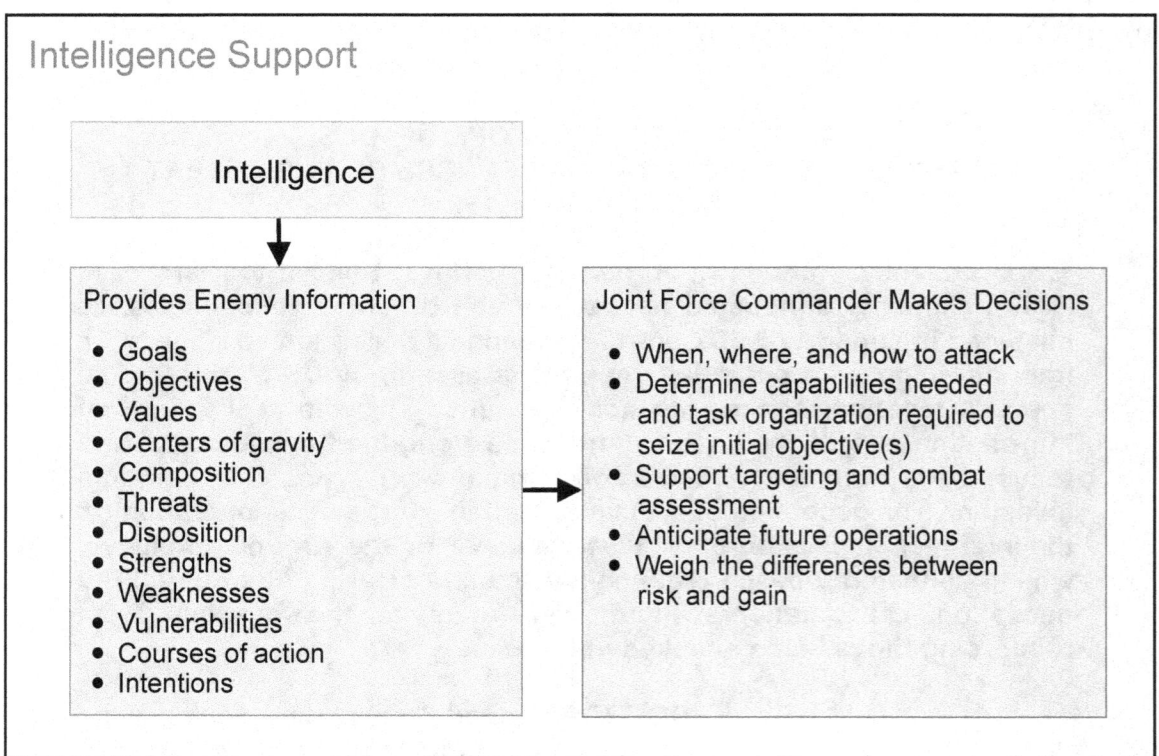

Figure IV-3. Intelligence Support

See JP 2-01, Joint and National Intelligence Support to Military Operations, *to identify the primary providers of intelligence assigned to or supporting the JFC, and the diverse products and services available to satisfy joint force intelligence requirements.*

b. Intelligence considerations for the five phases of a forcible entry operation are described below.

(1) **Preparation and Deployment (Phase I). Specific considerations during this phase include the following:**

(a) **Establishing the Intelligence Architecture.** The intelligence architecture must be **capable of supporting joint forces en route to and within the operational area.** Architecture planning must consider establishing connectivity over long distances between the joint force, the supporting theater joint intelligence operations center, and other defense and national intelligence organizations (to include federated intelligence partners) outside the operational area.

(b) **Joint Intelligence Preparation of the Operational Environment.** JIPOE is a key input to mission analysis and the process continues to refine and update intelligence products to provide commanders and staffs the means to successfully prosecute operations.

For further guidance on intelligence support, refer to JP 2-0, Joint Intelligence, *JP 2-01,* Joint and National Intelligence Support to Military Operations, *and JP 2-01.3,* Joint Intelligence Preparation of the Operational Environment.

(2) **Assault (Phase II).** The joint force is most vulnerable to enemy action during the assault phase. Effective indications and warnings, targeting support, and collection management of ISR assets to track enemy reaction to the assault and force protection are paramount concerns during this phase.

(3) **Stabilization of the Lodgment (Phase III) and Introduction of Follow-on Forces (Phase IV).** In the remaining phases of the operation, **intelligence assets within the lodgment increase in numbers and contribute to an enhanced collective intelligence capability.** If the joint force headquarters deploys into the lodgment, the J-2 must ensure the availability of sufficient assets to assure uninterrupted intelligence support to the joint force. The J-2 should anticipate an increase in the demand for human intelligence and CI assets to **conduct interrogation, intelligence collection, document and materiel exploitation,** and **support liaison** with the host nation country team and with any multinational forces introduced into the lodgment.

(4) **Termination or Transition Operations (Phase V)**

(a) **Termination of Operations. Intelligence assets continue to support the JFC's operations requirements and address the potential for resurgent hostilities** by either conventional or unconventional forces. Intelligence support may be required for such activities as minefield clearing, infrastructure reconstruction, foreign humanitarian assistance (FHA), or restoring civil law and order, while continuing the key task of intelligence support to force protection.

(b) **Transition to Follow-on Operations.** Once a forcible entry has been successfully executed as the first phase of a larger campaign, **the JFC shifts the focus of intelligence support from establishing the lodgment to sustained operations.** Intelligence support for sustained operations, planned during the initial phase of the operation and continually refined as the forcible entry operation progresses, now allows for a seamless transition that allows the JFC to begin execution of the specific sequel that will achieve campaign objectives. In some instances, follow-on operations will be in the form of stability operations or other forms of civil-military actions. These operations encompass a variety of activities that **vary in their respective intelligence support requirements.** Some operations such as a show of force, attacks and raids, and noncombatant evacuations may require the same level of support demanded by combat operations. Other operations such as FHA or counterdrug operations may not involve large scale combat, but will, nevertheless, still require intelligence support to plan and execute.

8. Information Operations

IO are integral to successful military operations and are key during forcible entry operations. The full impact of IO on friendly, neutral, and hostile forces should be considered with the key goal of IO achieving and maintaining information superiority for the US and its allies; and exploiting enemy information vulnerabilities. IO are the integrated employment, during military operations, of information-related capabilities in concert with other lines of operation to influence, disrupt, corrupt, or usurp the decision making of adversaries and potential adversaries while protecting our own. Supporting information-related capabilities (information assurance, physical security, physical attack, CI, and combat camera) have military purposes other than IO, but either operate in the information environment or have impact on the information environment.

See JP 3-13, Information Operations, *for more information.*

OPERATIONS SECURITY FAILURE—SOMALIA, 1992

In 1992, the United States committed forces to Somalia in response to devastating famine, made much worse by civil war and the complete collapse of the Somalia government. The initial forces committed by Joint Task Force RESTORE HOPE were special operations forces (SOF) reconnaissance teams preceding the landing force onto designated beaches. As they emerged from the water onto the beach, the SOF elements were surrounded by reporters and cameras, together with video crews and flood lighting. Not only were the reconnaissance teams exposed and pinpointed; they were blinded and restricted as they attempted to complete their mission.

Various Sources

---

a. IO is a key part of setting the conditions for forcible entry operational success; IO efforts will be central to achieving surprise and isolating the lodgment and will also be an important enabler for gaining control of the operational environment and neutralizing enemy forces. OPSEC and MILDEC, combined with the other information-related capabilities will be the heart of achieving operational and tactical surprise during the forcible entry operation.

(1) OPSEC attempts to **deny critical information about friendly forces to the adversary.** Forcible entry forces preparing for deployment have large, distinct signatures. **Masking the movement** of forces to staging bases and to the operational area is **critical to ensure OPSEC.** These movements may not be totally hidden; however, such detail as the composition of the forces or the time and location of the forcible entry should be concealed. The object is to surprise, confuse, or paralyze the enemy. **OPSEC procedures must be planned, practiced, and enforced** during training, movement, and operations.

For further details on OPSEC, refer to JP 3-13.3, Operations Security.

(2) MILDEC misleads adversary decision makers as to friendly military capabilities, intentions, and operations, thereby causing the adversary to take specific actions (or inactions) that will contribute to the accomplishment of the friendly mission. MILDEC operations should be closely coordinated with the overall operational scheme of maneuver. The deception operation will have little effect if it is compromised by poor OPSEC or conflicts with concurrent military information support operations. Successful MILDECs require sufficient resources, leadership, and linked objectives and goals from the strategic to tactical level. For forcible entry operations, **MILDEC operations may be planned and executed to complete the following:**

(a) Deceive the enemy as to the time, location(s), and strategic and/or operational purpose of the forcible entry.

(b) Focus enemy attention and effort away from actual assault objectives.

(c) Cause the enemy to disperse forces to defend all possible airheads and beachheads in the operational area so the enemy cannot mass decisive force to deny joint force assaults.

(d) Induce the enemy to piecemeal resources.

(e) Desensitize the enemy to US actions by appearances of "routine" activities.

(f) Force the enemy to maintain heightened states of alert and/or readiness for extended periods of time.

For further details on MILDEC, refer to JP 3-13.4, Military Deception.

b. Information-related capabilities will also play an integral role in isolating the lodgment. The lodgment must not only be isolated from nearby enemy military forces, but also from C2 centers outside the operational area. CO and EW, supported by physical attack on C2 networks, will play a decisive role in this isolation.

c. EW includes any military action involving the use of electromagnetic and directed energy to control the electromagnetic spectrum or to attack the enemy. The JFC's plan must be developed to ensure **complementary use of assets and weapons systems to effectively disrupt and/or destroy enemy C2 and weapons systems,** while protecting joint force capabilities.

See JP 3-13.1, Electronic Warfare, *for additional detail on EW.*

d. **Other Information-Related Capabilities**

(1) **Defense Support to Public Diplomacy.** DSPD consists of activities and measures taken by DOD components, not solely in the area of IO, to support and facilitate public diplomacy efforts of the US Government. DSPD requires coordination with both the interagency and among DOD components.

(2) **Public Affairs.** A PA plan should be prepared during the planning process and executed upon initiation of the forcible entry operation. PA planning must anticipate detection of all but small covert operations by the enemy and the press.

JP 3-61, Public Affairs, *provides additional guidance on incorporating PA into the planning process.*

(3) **Civil-Military Operations.** Properly executed CMO during forcible entry operations can reduce potential friction points between the civilian population and the joint force, specifically by eliminating interference with military operations and limiting the impact of military operations on the populace. **CMO** encompass the activities taken by a commander to establish and maintain effective relations between military forces and civil authorities, the general population, and other civil institutions in friendly, neutral, or hostile areas where those forces are employed. Use of civil affairs (CA) forces and units specifically organized, trained, and equipped to conduct CA operations in support of CMO can assist the commander.

For further details on CMO, refer to JP 3-57, Civil-Military Operations.

9. **Chemical, Biological, Radiological, and Nuclear Considerations**

While the enemy may employ CBRN weapons at any point in the conflict, forces are especially vulnerable to CBRN attack during phase II and phase III operations. Planning against an enemy known to have the capability and willingness to employ CBRN weapons/devices should take into account the need for protective clothing, decontamination, and logistical support to enable the force to continue the mission. Additional considerations may include the need for specialized training for the assault forces, or the need for additional CBRN units to further support operations.

Additional guidance may be found in JP 3-11, Operations in Chemical, Biological, Radiological, and Nuclear (CBRN) Environments, *and JP 3-40,* Combating Weapons of Mass Destruction.

Intentionally Blank

CHAPTER V
LOGISTICS

1. General

As applied to military operations and forcible entry operations specifically, logistic services comprise the support capabilities that collectively enable the US to rapidly provide sustainment for military forces in order to achieve the envisioned end state of the operation or larger campaign (see Figure V-1). This requires commanders to plan and establish the logistic systems that flow sufficient logistics through the lodgment(s) created to support follow-on operations. Logistic planning must account for early resupply of initial assault forces as these forces will generally be employed with limited on-hand capacities.

For additional information on deployment and redeployment planning, see JP 3-35, Deployment and Redeployment Operations, *and for logistic consideration, planning, and execution, see the JP 4-0 Series.*

2. Specific Logistic Considerations for Supporting Forcible Entry Operations

Logistic planning for the phases of forcible entry operations occurs concurrently, not sequentially. Planning should address the logistic core capabilities as identified in Figure V-2.

Logistics Planning Considerations

- Geography
- Transportation Considerations
- Logistic Capabilities
- Logistic Enhancements
- Multinational Support
- Contractor Support
- Protection of Logistics
- Responsive Echeloned Support

- Assignment of Responsibility
- Risk Analysis
- Demands of an Expanding Force
- Critical Items
- System Constraints
- Movement Control
- Resupply Systems
- Intermediate Staging Base

Figure V-1. Logistics Planning Considerations

Logistic Core Capabilities

- Supply Operations
- Maintenance Operations
- Deployment and Distribution
- Health Services

- Engineering
- Logistics Services
- Operational Contract Support

Figure V-2. Logistic Core Capabilities

The following specific planning considerations supplement those detailed in JP 4-0, *Joint Logistics*, and JP 5-0, *Joint Operation Planning*.

a. **Phase I (Preparation and Deployment)**

(1) Identify and coordinate for ISBs as required.

(2) Identify time-phased logistic requirements.

(3) Develop prioritized transportation requirements.

(4) Analyze capabilities, limitations, and vulnerabilities of APODs and APOEs, SPODs and SPOEs, coastal areas for JLOTS, and operational area infrastructure to support projected operations.

(5) Determine air, land, and sea LOC requirements to support forcible entry and subsequent operations.

(6) Determine logistic factors and establish airhead and beachhead resupply responsibility.

(7) Analyze force health protection and health service support planning considerations.

(8) Analyze and/or assess multinational support and contractor capabilities to support operations.

(9) Analyze and recommend changes to TPFDL flow to ensure that adequate support will be available.

(10) Integrate and synchronize logistic support of initial and subsequent flow of forces into the operational area.

b. **Phase II (Assault)**

(1) Analyze potential lodgment area to ensure continuous air and sea landing of personnel, equipment, and logistic resources, as well as availability of facilities.

(2) Provide adequate medical support and evacuation to support concurrent or integrated assaults by amphibious, airborne, air assault, and SOF.

c. **Phase III (Stabilization of the Lodgment)**

(1) Project and/or resolve restrictions and/or limitations in the capability to support force flow.

(2) Determine means of delivery and capacities to maximize combat power.

(3) Identify and plan advanced logistic bases in support of the joint force operational concept. Unless additional forcible entry operations are anticipated, planning for follow-on operations will be in accordance with standard joint force logistic planning doctrine in JP 4-0, *Joint Logistics.*

(4) Seek methods to maximize and expand throughput capabilities of APODs and SPODs.

(5) Develop provisions to clear reinforcing supplies and equipment from off-load points.

(6) Analyze requirements to expand the lodgment with regard to maximum on ground capabilities, throughput, and infrastructure.

d. **Phase IV (Introduction of Follow-on Forces)**

(1) Identify mission support requirements for follow-on operations.

(2) Begin MPF and APS afloat operations.

(3) Continue buildup of preplanned supplies.

(4) Initiate general engineering and construction plans for support to follow-on operations.

(5) Plan for reconstitution and redeployment of the assault force for follow-on operations.

e. **Phase V (Termination or Transition Operations)**

(1) Redeploy and/or reconstitute assault forces as appropriate.

(2) Plan for preparing the force for follow-on, out-of-area operations, such as redeployment to another geographical area.

(3) Once plans have formally addressed and integrated all seven core logistic capabilities, the force should be well prepared to begin the application of those functions that support operational execution (see Figure V-2).

APPENDIX A
AMPHIBIOUS ASSAULT OPERATIONS

1. Purpose

This appendix provides an overview of amphibious assault operations.

2. Amphibious Assaults

An amphibious assault involves the establishment of an LF on a hostile or potentially hostile shore. The organic capabilities of AFs, including air and fire support, logistics, and mobility, allow them to gain access to an area by forcible entry. The salient requirement of an amphibious assault is the necessity for swift buildup of sufficient combat power ashore, from an initial zero capability to full coordinated striking power, as the attack progresses toward AF objectives. The assault begins on order, after sufficient elements of the main body of the AF that are capable of beginning the ship-to-shore movement arrive in the operational area. For an assault, the action phase ends when conditions specified in the initiating directive are met, as recommended by the CATF and CLF and approved by the JFC or designated commander. Amphibious assaults are used, for example, to initiate a campaign or major operation, such as the 1942 landing on Guadalcanal, which began the campaign to neutralize the enemy base at Rabaul in the Southwest Pacific, or the 1944 Normandy landings that established a beachhead for the Allied campaign across Western Europe.

a. **Characteristics.** Factors that influence a commander's decision to select an amphibious assault as the type of forcible entry operation to be conducted include its mobility, flexibility in task organization, ability to rapidly build up combat power ashore, and sustainability. Amphibious assault operations can exploit the element of surprise and capitalize on enemy weakness by projecting combat power at the most advantageous location and time. As with other types of forcible entry operations, the threat of an amphibious assault can induce enemies to divert forces, establish or reinforce defensive positions, divert major resources, or disperse forces.

b. **Amphibious Force Composition.** An AF is composed of an ATF and an LF together with other forces that are trained, organized, and equipped for amphibious operations.

For detailed information on amphibious assaults and other amphibious operations, see JP 3-02, Amphibious Operations.

Intentionally Blank

APPENDIX B
AIRBORNE AND AIR ASSAULT OPERATIONS

1. Purpose

This appendix provides an overview of airborne and air assault operations.

2. Airborne and Air Assault Operations

Joint airborne and air assault operations involve the air movement and delivery of specially trained combat forces and logistic support into an objective area to execute a mission. Airborne and air assault forces provide the commander with the unique ability to quickly respond on short notice and mass rapidly on critical targets. Airborne operations are executed by specially trained forces and can be launched at a considerable distance from the target area with such speed as to cause tactical or operational surprise and prevent effective action by the enemy. Airborne forces can secure and/or destroy critical installations, facilities or terrain; reinforce US and multinational forces; and conduct a show of force or attack an adversary in isolated areas. Air assault operations increase mobility and freedom of action by providing operational and tactical mobility for both the offense and defense. Air operations enable forces to reduce time and space limitations normally encountered in movement of assault forces by land, cross terrain obstacles, bypass hostile areas, and attack, destroy, and/or seize objectives deep in enemy territory. Each component can significantly contribute to the successful execution of airborne and air assault operations.

a. **Concept.** Airborne and air assault forces are capable of conducting operations in support of strategic, operational, and tactical objectives. They land intact with weapons, ammunition, and other combat equipment and are prepared for combat immediately. Airborne forces aggressively seize and hold objectives until linkup is accomplished. An airborne operation usually terminates upon seizure of the objective, linkup with other ground forces, or extraction. Air assault operations are deliberate, precisely planned, and vigorously executed to strike over extended distances.

b. **Characteristics.** Airborne and air assault forces share many of the same capabilities. They can extend the battlefield, move, and rapidly concentrate combat power quicker than land forces. Airborne and air assault forces also share the same limitations. They are dependent on the availability of airlift assets, fire support, and combat service support resources; they are highly vulnerable to enemy attack by ground and air forces while en route to the LZ and/or DZ; and are equally assailable when operating in open terrain against an armored threat or WMD. Environmental conditions and adverse weather can also impact performance. There are four phases of airborne operations: marshalling, air movement, landing, and ground tactical phases. Air assault operations have five phases: staging, loading, air movement, landing, and ground tactical phases.

3. Organization and Command

a. **Planning.** From the time an operation is announced until it is completed or terminated, echelons of participating components coordinate continuously. The commander, joint task force (CJTF) initiates airborne and/or air assault operations with a planning directive to participating units. The directive is distributed through normal command channels, and pertinent information is issued to subordinate units. After receipt of a directive and preparation of initial estimates and studies, the commanders, staffs, and representatives of supporting forces meet in a joint conference to develop a CONOPS. The CONOPS forms the basis for the preparation of the commander's planning directive and development of OPLANs and OPORDs, including a list of forces in support, a schedule of events, and stated conditions under which the operation will begin, be delayed, altered, or terminated.

b. **Coordination.** Airborne and air assault commanders begin planning operations with a visualization of the ground tactical plan and work through a reverse-planning sequence. Planning for airborne and air assault operations is as detailed as time permits. For airborne operations, this sequence includes the development of a ground tactical plan, landing plan, air movement plan, and marshalling plan. For air assault operations the sequence is the same, but instead of a marshalling plan, loading and staging plans are developed. Direct liaison and coordination between the logistic support agencies of the participating components and other supporting forces occur during the preliminary planning stages. For airborne and air assault operations, intelligence systems assist in accomplishing strategic objectives, including all factors which will impact the arrival of forces into the objective area, establishment of airheads and lodgments, and linkup of forces in preparation for follow-on operations. Also included in the planning process are the following: counterair, IO, logistics, joint fire support, force protection, SO, engineer support, PA, and military police. When developing the OPLAN, the JFC anticipates that assault forces may face natural and man-made obstacles that are intended to restrict their movement so that the enemy can mass its forces and repel the assault. Combat engineers facilitate insertion of assault forces and prepare the onward movement to the objective by clearing breaches, roads, and airfields of mines and obstacles.

c. **Command.** The JFC may initiate joint airborne and/or air assault operations in support of strategic and/or operational objectives. The complexity of airborne and air assault operations and their vulnerability require an exceptional degree of unity of effort and operational coherence. The initiating directive is an order to the airborne and/or air assault commander to conduct the operation. It is issued by the JFC delegated overall authority for the operation. JFCs establish command relationships and assign authority to subordinates based on the operational situation, the complexity of the mission, and the degree of control needed to ensure that strategic intent is satisfied.

d. **Control.** Airspace C2, established boundaries, ability to communicate, and the effective employment of surveillance, reconnaissance, and EW are key elements in facilitating effective C2 of airborne and air assault operations. The airborne force commander establishes a standard C2 system by defining the functions and responsibilities of key personnel, ensuring that all preliminary operational planning is accomplished, and publishing OPLANs and orders. Air assault operations feature extended distances and speed of execution. To work swiftly under pressure, efforts must be integrated and synchronized. Effective liaison between operational elements of an airborne and/or air assault operation and with higher authorities will facilitate mutual understanding, unity of purpose, and unity of action.

e. **Command and Control of Airborne Operations**. Airborne assault, particularly over intercontinental distance, places additional requirements on C2. En route mission planning and rehearsal systems allow the airborne force to maintain situational awareness and to receive and disseminate updated intelligence while en route from load time at the APOE until arrival over the airhead.

(1) The airborne assault force commander accompanies the initial assault and is responsible for (see Figure B-1 for a list of tasks at various command levels):

(a) Ground tactical planning.

(b) Rig and out load troopers and equipment.

(c) En route mission planning and rehearsal.

(d) Conduct airborne assault.

(e) Seize assault objectives.

(f) Execute joint fires.

(g) Update the intelligence preparation of the battlespace.

(h) Secure the APOD.

(i) Repair and maintain the APOD.

(j) Expand the lodgment.

(2) The airborne task force commander may also be the JTF or land component commander, depending upon experience and the scope of the operation. If the assault requires an airborne BCT, for example, the BCT commander leads the assault force, and the parent Army headquarters (normally a division) provides the airborne task force commander. This ensures that the assault force commander can give his full attention to the fight in the airhead and not be consumed with managing en route follow-on forces and support.

(3) Initially, the airborne task force commander exercises control from an airborne command post outside the airhead or from a secure base with linkages to the airhead and all

Example Distribution of Responsibilities for Airborne Assault

	Planning and Preparation	Assault	Follow-on Operations
Joint Task Force (JTF) Headquarters	Operational planning Develop time-phased force and deployment data Intelligence, surveillance, and reconnaissance planning and integration Joint shaping operations Special operations forces integration Military deception Exercise of command and control (C2) over intermediate staging base	C2 of supported and supporting components Go/no go decision Modify force flow based on situation Apportion and allocate joint support	Control flow of joint forces
Airborne Task Force Headquarters	Tactical planning Integrate joint fires Integrate long range surveillance and special operations forces operations Control pre-assault fires Rig and load personnel and equipment	En route C2 and airspace command and control C2 relay between JTF and assault force Expand C2 network on the ground	Assume overall command of ground forces Reception, staging, and onward movement for follow-on ground forces
Assault Force Headquarters	Develop ground plan and rehearse ground operations En route planning Seize assault objectives Secure and defend airhead Control supporting fires	En route planning Seize assault objectives Secure and defend airhead Control supporting fires	Expand lodgment Receive initial follow-on forces Link-up with special operations forces and amph bious forces Exploitation

Figure B-1. Example Distribution of Responsibilities for Airborne Assault

joint supporting assets. The airborne task force commander's responsibilities include operational planning, APOE situational awareness and integration, en route C2, aerial relay using joint communications, integrate joint fires, integrate long range surveillance and SOF, C2 pre-assault fires, C2 the APOE and APOD, C2 of reception, staging, and onward movement of follow-on forces. After the airhead is secure, the airborne task force commander moves into the lodgment and assumes command of the assault force and follow-on forces.

(4) The CJTF is responsible for joint operational planning, joint integrated prioritized target list development, joint ISR integration, setting the conditions for joint forcible entry, C2, and air flow and air space management.

f. Forces

(1) US Army airborne forces are committed to combat by parachute assault, air landed operations, or by a combination of these two methods. Normally, airborne operations are initiated by parachute assault conducted by an airborne infantry BCT. Parachute assault permits delivery of combined arms teams into the airhead in less time than air landed operations require. Once the assault phase is initiated, it is followed by one or more of the following: a defensive phase; an offensive phase; or an extraction phase.

(2) The initial assault stresses the coordinated action of small units to seize initial objectives before the advantage of surprise has worn off. After the initial assault landings accomplish the initial ground missions, commanders must organize the airhead line. Airborne forces defend to protect and retain areas or installations seized during the assault phase of the operation. Because an airborne assault is most often conducted in the enemy rear, an all-around defense is required. Units can be airlanded on terrain under the control of friendly forces near the line of contact or on secured locations in the enemy's rear; however, it takes time to land a sizable force and a secured LZ is necessary. Even when multiple LZs are employed, it takes longer to mass forces in the airhead during airland operations than during parachute operations. Subsequent operations can include continued defense of the airhead, linkup, passage of lines, relief, withdrawal, or offensive operations, to include exploitation or further airborne and/or air assaults.

(3) Air Assault. Whether performed from the sea or a land ISB, aviation and combined arms provide the JFC with an agile fighting force capable of conducting both offensive and defensive operations. Air assault operations allow friendly forces to strike over extended distances and terrain barriers to attack the enemy when and where he is most vulnerable. Air assaults are deliberately planned due to their complex nature; however, units are often required to execute air assaults within short time constraints. Reinforcement of committed units, linkup operations, gap crossing operations, security operations, limited visibility operations, and ship-to-shore operations should all be considered during air assault operations.

(4) Sustainment. Minimum sustainment elements accompany airborne forces into the airhead or lodgment. They perform most essential services in the marshalling area or they defer them. Sustainment is normally divided into three echelons during deployment: assault, follow-on, and rear echelons. Sustainment of these forces is helped by distribution of supplies, resupply by air including planned resupply, immediate airdrop resupply, and emergency airdrop resupply requests; maintenance during airborne operations; transportation; and health services support. The air assault force is supported by both organic and external elements organized to push supplies, materiel, fuel, and ammunition forward by air. The exact organization and disposition of the assault and follow-on sustainment elements is a function of the air assault force's mission and anticipated follow-on operations.

4. Termination or Transition

a. Airborne/air assault operations will normally transition combat operations to follow-on forces. However, the JFC should prepare contingency plans for the possibility that follow-on forces are unable to relieve the airborne/air assault force. The follow-on operation would be one of the following:

(1) Withdrawal or evacuation of units.

(2) Linkup with ground forces.

(3) Exfiltration.

(4) Breakout from encirclement.

b. As conditions permit, the build up of forces and supplies continues and follow-on operations commence. The airfield transitions from being seized to being improved for use as an airbase suitable for joint operations.

Army Field Manual (FM) 90-26, Airborne Operations, *provides more specifics on airborne and air assault operations.*

APPENDIX C
REFERENCES

The development of JP 3-18 is based upon the following primary references:

1. Department of Defense Publications

DOD Directive 5100.01, *Functions of the Department of Defense and Its Major Components.*

2. Chairman of the Joint Chiefs of Staff Publications

a. CJCSI 3110.10E, *Communication Systems Supplement to the Joint Strategic Capabilities Plan (JSCP) FY10.*

b. CJCSI 3121.01B, *Standing Rules of Engagement/Standing Rules for the Use of Force for US Forces.*

c. CJCSI 5120.02C, *Joint Doctrine Development System.*

d. Chairman of the Joint Chiefs of Staff Manual (CJCSM) 3122.01A, *Joint Operation Planning and Execution System (JOPES) Volume I, Planning Policies and Procedures.*

e. CJCSM 3122.02D, Joint Operation Planning and Execution System (*JOPES*) *Volume III, Time-Phased Force and Deployment Data Development and Deployment Execution.*

f. CJCSM 3122.03C, *Joint Operation Planning and Execution System (JOPES) Volume II, Planning Formats.*

g. JP 1, *Doctrine for the Armed Forces of the United States.*

h. JP 1-02, *Department of Defense Dictionary of Military and Associated Terms.*

i. JP 2-01, *Joint and National Intelligence Support to Military Operations.*

j. JP 2-01.3, *Joint Intelligence Preparation of the Operational Environment.*

k. JP 3-0, *Joint Operations.*

l. JP 3-01, *Countering Air and Missile Threats.*

m. JP 3-02, *Amphibious Operations.*

n. JP 3-02.1, *Amphibious Embarkation and Debarkation.*

o. JP 3-03, *Joint Interdiction.*

p. JP 3-05, *Special Operations.*

q. JP 3-09, *Joint Fire Support.*

r. JP 3-09.3, *Close Air Support.*

s. JP 3-10, *Joint Security Operations in Theater.*

t. JP 3-11, *Operations in Chemical, Biological, Radiological, and Nuclear (CBRN) Environments.*

u. JP 3-12, *Cyberspace Operations.*

v. JP 3-13, *Information Operations.*

w. JP 3-13.1, *Electronic Warfare.*

x. JP 3-13.2, *Military Information Support Operations.*

y. JP 3-13.3, *Operations Security.*

z. JP 3-13.4, *Military Deception.*

aa. JP 3-15, *Barriers, Obstacles, and Mine Warfare for Joint Operations.*

bb. JP 3-17, *Air Mobility Operations.*

cc. JP 3-30, *Command and Control for Joint Air Operations.*

dd. JP 3-31, *Command and Control for Joint Land Operations.*

ee. JP 3-32, *Command and Control for Joint Maritime Operations.*

ff. JP 3-33, *Joint Task Force Headquarters.*

gg. JP 3-34, *Joint Engineer Operations.*

hh. JP 3-35, *Deployment and Redeployment Operations.*

ii. JP 3-40, *Combating Weapons of Mass Destruction.*

jj. JP 3-52, *Joint Airspace Control.*

kk. JP 3-57, *Civil-Military Operations.*

ll. JP 3-61, *Public Affairs.*

mm. JP 4-0, *Joint Logistics.*

nn. JP 4-01.6, *Joint Logistics Over-the-Shore.*

oo. JP 4-02, *Health Service Support.*

pp. JP 4-06, *Mortuary Affairs.*

qq. JP 5-0, *Joint Operation Planning.*

rr. JP 6-0, *Joint Communications System.*

3. Multi-Service Publications

Field Manual (FM) 3-52.2/Marine Corps Reference Publication (MCRP) 3-25F/Navy Tactics, Techniques, and Procedures (NTTP) 3-56.2/Air Force Tactics, Techniques, and Procedures (Instruction) (AFTTP[I]) 3-2.17, *TAGS: Multi-Service Tactics, Techniques, and Procedures for the Theater Air-Ground System.*

4. US Army Publications

a. FM 3-0, *Operations.*

b. FM 3-05, *Army Special Operations Forces.*

c. FM 4-0, *Sustainment.*

d. FM 90-26, *Airborne Operations.*

5. US Naval Publications

a. Naval Doctrine Publication 1, *Naval Warfare.*

b. NTTP 3-02.2, *Supporting Arms in Amphibious Operations.*

6. US Marine Corps Publications

a. Marine Corps Doctrinal Publication (MCDP) 1-1, *Strategy.*

b. MCDP 1-2, *Campaigning.*

c. MCDP 1-3, *Tactics.*

d. MCDP 3, *Expeditionary Operations.*

e. MCDP 6, *Command and Control.*

f. *Marine Corps Capabilities Plan.*

7. US Air Force Publications

a. Air Force Doctrine Document (AFDD) 1, *Air Force Basic Doctrine, Organization, and Command.*

b. AFDD 2-0, *Global Integrated Intelligence, Surveillance, and Reconnaissance Operations.*

c. AFDD 3-01, *Counterair Operations.*

d. AFDD 3-05, *Special Operations.*

e. AFDD 3-03, *Counterland Operations.*

f. AFDD 3-14, *Engineer Operations.*

APPENDIX D
ADMINISTRATIVE INSTRUCTIONS

1. User Comments

Users in the field are highly encouraged to submit comments on this publication to: Joint Staff J-7, Joint Education and Doctrine Division (JEDD), Pentagon, Room 2D763, Washington, DC, 20318-7000. These comments should address content (accuracy, usefulness, consistency, and organization), writing, and appearance.

2. Authorship

The lead agent for this publication is the US Army. The Joint Staff doctrine sponsor for this publication is the Director for Operational Plans and Joint Force Development (J-7).

3. Supersession

This publication supersedes JP 3-18, 16 June 2008, *Joint Forcible Entry Operations*.

4. Change Recommendations

a. Recommendations for urgent changes to this publication should be submitted:

    TO: JOINT STAFF WASHINGTON DC//J7-JEDD//

Routine changes should be submitted electronically to the Deputy Director, Joint and Coalition Warfighting, Joint and Coalition Warfighting Center, Joint Doctrine Support Division and info the lead agent and the Director for Joint Force Development, J-7/JEDD.

b. When a Joint Staff directorate submits a proposal to the Chairman of the Joint Chiefs of Staff that would change source document information reflected in this publication, that directorate will include a proposed change to this publication as an enclosure to its proposal. The Services and other organizations are requested to notify the Joint Staff J-7 when changes to source documents reflected in this publication are initiated.

5. Distribution of Publications

Local reproduction is authorized, and access to unclassified publications is unrestricted. However, access to, and reproduction authorization for, classified joint publications must be in accordance with DOD Manual 5200.01, Volume 1, *DOD Information Security Program: Overview, Classification, and Declassification,* and DOD Manual 5200.01, Volume 3, *DOD Information Security Program: Protection of Classified Information.*

6. Distribution of Electronic Publications

a. Joint Staff J-7 will not print copies of JPs for distribution. Electronic versions are available on JDEIS at https://jdeis.js.mil (NIPRNET) and http://jdeis.js.smil.mil (SIPRNET), and on the JEL at http://www.dtic.mil/doctrine (NIPRNET).

b. Only approved JPs and joint test publications are releasable outside the combatant commands, Services, and Joint Staff. Release of any classified JP to foreign governments or foreign nationals must be requested through the local embassy (Defense Attaché Office) to DIA, Defense Foreign Liaison/IE-3, 200 MacDill Blvd., Joint Base Anacostia-Bolling, Washington, DC 20340-5100.

c. JEL CD-ROM. Upon request of a joint doctrine development community member, the Joint Staff J-7 will produce and deliver one CD-ROM with current JPs. This JEL CD-ROM will be updated not less than semi-annually and when received can be locally reproduced for use within the combatant commands and Services.

GLOSSARY
PART I—ABBREVIATIONS AND ACRONYMS

AADC	area air defense commander
AAGS	Army air-ground system
ACA	airspace control authority
AF	amphibious force
AFDD	Air Force doctrine document
AO	area of operations
AOA	amphibious objective area
APOD	aerial port of debarkation
APOE	aerial port of embarkation
APS	Army pre-positioned stocks
ATF	amphibious task force
BCT	brigade combat team
C2	command and control
CA	civil affairs
CAF	commander, airborne/air assault force
CAP	crisis action planning
CAS	close air support
CATF	commander, amphibious task force
CBRN	chemical, biological, radiological, and nuclear
CCDR	combatant commander
CCG	combat communications group
CDRJSOTF	commander, joint special operations task force
CI	counterintelligence
CJCSI	Chairman of the Joint Chiefs of Staff instruction
CJCSM	Chairman of the Joint Chiefs of Staff manual
CJTF	commander, joint task force
CLF	commander, landing force
CMO	civil-military operations
CO	cyberspace operations
COA	course of action
CONOPS	concept of operations
CONPLAN	concept plan
CONUS	continental United States
CRG	contingency response group
DOD	Department of Defense
DSPD	defense support to public diplomacy
DZ	drop zone
EW	electronic warfare

FHA	foreign humanitarian assistance
FM	field manual (Army)
FSCM	fire support coordination measure
GCC	geographic combatant commander
HIDACZ	high-density airspace control zone
IO	information operations
ISB	intermediate staging base
ISR	intelligence, surveillance, and reconnaissance
J-2	intelligence directorate of a joint staff
J-6	communications system directorate of a joint staff
JFACC	joint force air component commander
JFC	joint force commander
JFLCC	joint force land component commander
JFMCC	joint force maritime component commander
JIPOE	joint intelligence preparation of the operational environment
JLOTS	joint logistics over-the-shore
JOPES	Joint Operation Planning and Execution System
JOPP	joint operation planning process
JP	joint publication
JSOA	joint special operations area
JTF	joint task force
LF	landing force
LOC	line of communications
LZ	landing zone
MCDP	Marine Corps doctrine publication
MCM	mine countermeasures
MILDEC	military deception
MPF	maritime pre-positioning force
NSFS	naval surface fire support
NTTP	Navy tactics, techniques, and procedures
OPLAN	operation plan
OPORD	operation order
OPSEC	operations security
PA	public affairs
RADC	regional air defense commander
ROE	rules of engagement

SADC	sector air defense commander
SATCOM	satellite communications
SecDef	Secretary of Defense
SLOC	sea line of communications
SO	special operations
SOF	special operations forces
SPOD	seaport of debarkation
SPOE	seaport of embarkation
STT	special tactics team
TACS	theater air control system
TACSAT	tactical satellite
TF	task force
TPFDL	time-phased force and deployment list
TSOC	theater special operations command
UHF	ultrahigh frequency
UW	unconventional warfare
WMD	weapons of mass destruction

air assault. The movement of friendly assault forces by rotary-wing aircraft to engage and destroy enemy forces or to seize and hold key terrain. (Approved for incorporation into JP 1-02.)

air assault force. A force composed primarily of ground and rotary-wing air units organized, equipped, and trained for air assault operations. (JP 1-02. SOURCE: JP 3-18)

air assault operation. An operation in which assault forces, using the mobility of rotary-wing assets and the total integration of available firepower, maneuver under the control of a ground or air maneuver commander to engage enemy forces or to seize and hold key terrain. (Approved for incorporation into JP 1-02.)

airborne assault. The use of airborne forces to parachute into an objective area to attack and eliminate armed resistance and secure designated objectives. (Approved for incorporation into JP 1-02.)

airborne lift. None. (Approved for removal from JP 1-02.)

airborne operation. An operation involving the air movement into an objective area of combat forces and their logistic support for execution of a tactical, operational, or strategic mission. (Approved for incorporation into JP 1-02.)

airborne troops. None. (Approved for removal from JP 1-02.)

aircraft loading table. None. (Approved for removal from JP 1-02.)

airhead. 1. A designated area in a hostile or potentially hostile operational area that, when seized and held, ensures the continuous air landing of troops and materiel and provides the maneuver space necessary for projected operations. Also called **a lodgment area.** (JP 3-18) 2. A designated location in an operational area used as a base for supply and evacuation by air. (JP 3-17) (Approved for incorporation into JP 1-02.)

airhead line. A line denoting the limits of the objective area for an airborne assault. (Approved for incorporation into JP 1-02.)

assault. 1. In an amphibious operation, the period of time between the arrival of the major assault forces of the amphibious task force in the objective area and the accomplishment of the amphibious task force mission. (JP 3-02) 2. To make a short, violent, but well-ordered attack against a local objective, such as a gun emplacement, a fort, or a machine gun nest. (JP 3-18) 3. A phase of an airborne operation beginning with delivery by air of the assault echelon of the force into the objective area and extending through attack of assault objectives and consolidation of the initial airhead. (JP 3-18) (Approved for incorporation into JP 1-02.)

assault phase. In an airborne operation, a phase beginning with delivery by air of the assault echelon of the force into the objective area and extending through attack of assault objectives and consolidation of the initial airhead. (JP 1-02. SOURCE: JP 3-18.)

beach marker. None. (Approved for removal from JP 1-02.)

combined arms team. The full integration and application of two or more arms or elements of one Service into an operation. (Approved for incorporation into JP 1-02.)

covering force. 1. A force operating apart from the main force for the purpose of intercepting, engaging, delaying, disorganizing, and deceiving the enemy before the enemy can attack the force covered. 2. Any body or detachment of troops which provides security for a larger force by observation, reconnaissance, attack, or defense, or by any combination of these methods. (JP 1-02. SOURCE: JP 3-18)

forcible entry. Seizing and holding of a military lodgment in the face of armed opposition. (JP 1-02. SOURCE: JP 3-18)

initiating directive. An order to a subordinate commander to conduct military operations as directed. Also called **ID.** (Approved for incorporation into JP 1-02.)

lodgment. A designated area in a hostile or potentially hostile operational area that, when seized and held, makes the continuous landing of troops and materiel possible and provides maneuver space for subsequent operations. (JP 1-02. SOURCE: JP 3-18)

lodgment area. None. (Approved for removal from JP 1-02.)

Marine expeditionary brigade. None. (Approved for removal from JP 1-02.)

passage of lines. An operation in which a force moves forward or rearward through another force's combat positions with the intention of moving into or out of contact with the enemy. (Approved for incorporation into JP 1-02.)

seize. To employ combat forces to occupy physically and to control a designated area. (JP 1-02. SOURCE: JP 3-18)

staging base. 1. An advanced naval base for the anchoring, fueling, and refitting of transports and cargo ships as well as replenishment of mobile service squadrons. (JP 4-01.2) 2. A landing and takeoff area with minimum servicing, supply, and shelter provided for the temporary occupancy of military aircraft during the course of movement from one location to another. (JP 3-18) (Approved for incorporation into JP 1-02)

vertical envelopment. A tactical maneuver in which troops that are air-dropped, air-landed, or inserted via air assault, attack the rear and flanks of a force, in effect cutting off or encircling the force. (Approved for incorporation into JP 1-02.)

JOINT DOCTRINE PUBLICATIONS HIERARCHY

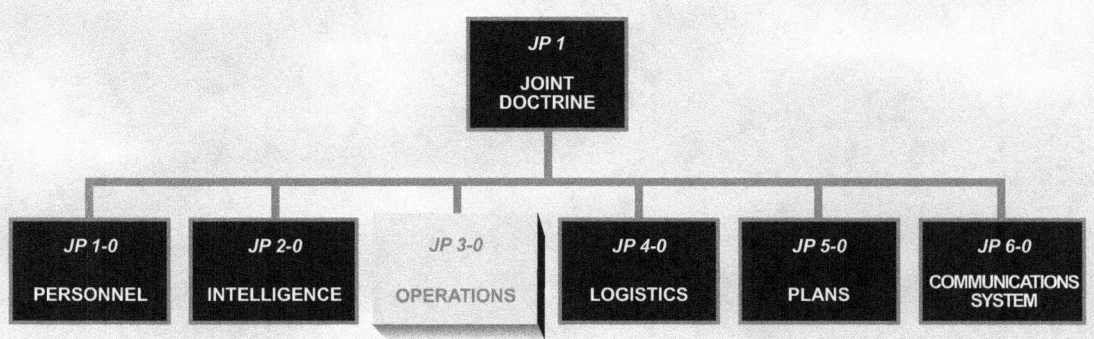

All joint publications are organized into a comprehensive hierarchy as shown in the chart above. **Joint Publication (JP) 3-18** is in the **Operations** series of joint doctrine publications. The diagram below illustrates an overview of the development process:

STEP #4 - Maintenance

- JP published and continuously assessed by users
- Formal assessment begins 24 27 months following publication
- Revision begins 3.5 years after publication
- Each JP revision is completed no later than 5 years after signature

STEP #1 - Initiation

- Joint doctrine development community (JDDC) submission to fill extant operational void
- Joint Staff (JS) J 7 conducts front end analysis
- Joint Doctrine Planning Conference validation
- Program directive (PD) development and staffing/joint working group
- PD includes scope, references, outline, milestones, and draft authorship
- JS J 7 approves and releases PD to lead agent (LA) (Service, combatant command, JS directorate)

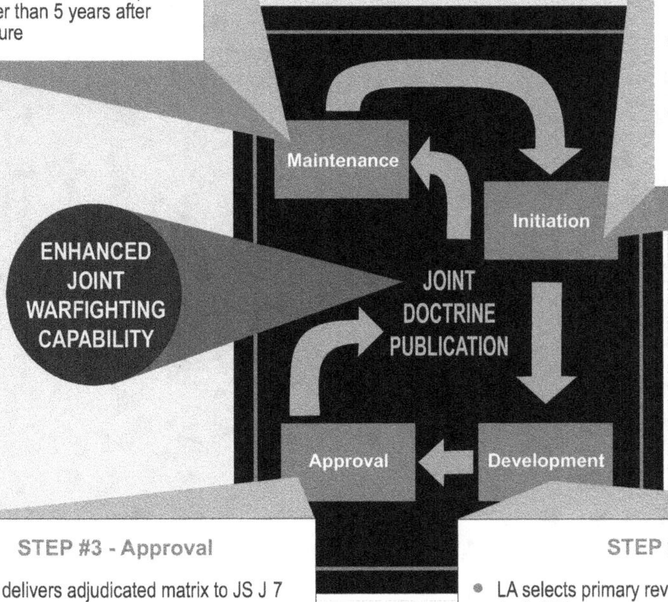

ENHANCED JOINT WARFIGHTING CAPABILITY

Maintenance

Initiation

JOINT DOCTRINE PUBLICATION

Approval

Development

STEP #3 - Approval

- JSDS delivers adjudicated matrix to JS J 7
- JS J 7 prepares publication for signature
- JSDS prepares JS staffing package
- JSDS staffs the publication via JSAP for signature

STEP #2 - Development

- LA selects primary review authority (PRA) to develop the first draft (FD)
- PRA develops FD for staffing with JDDC
- FD comment matrix adjudication
- JS J 7 produces the final coordination (FC) draft, staffs to JDDC and JS via Joint Staff Action Processing (JSAP) system
- Joint Staff doctrine sponsor (JSDS) adjudicates FC comment matrix
- FC joint working group